# Foreign Teaching Assistants in U.S. Universities

Kathleen M. Bailey
Frank Pialorsi
Jean Zukowski/Faust
Editors

National Association for Foreign Student Affairs
Washington, D.C. 1984

The National Association for Foreign Student Affairs is a nonprofit membership association that provides training, information, and other educational services to professionals in the field of international educational exchange. The membership is composed of more than 4,500 representatives of postsecondary institutions, school systems, community organizations, and educational associations. Members implement Association programs and participate in the determination of policies and activities through their Board of Directors and more than 35 committees, commissions, and special interest groups.

This book was sponsored by the NAFSA Field Service. Funded through a grant from the Student Support Services Division of the U.S. Information Agency, the Field Service seeks to strengthen services provided to foreign students at U.S. colleges and universities and to U.S. students abroad.

Copies of this publication can be ordered from the Publications Order Desk, National Association for Foreign Student Affairs, 1860 19th Street, N.W., Washington, D.C. 20009.

Library of Congress Catalog Card Number: 84-060503

ISBN: 0-912207-03-5

# Contents

# Acknowledgments

Many people have contributed to the production of this volume. The editors would particularly like to thank the chapter authors for their time and effort. Several of these chapters were originally papers given by the authors at academic conferences. They describe ground-breaking work which has since been replicated at several schools throughout the country. Over the last few years many other professionals who are not mentioned here by name have shared with us information about their efforts to help international teaching assistants.

In terms of the production process, this collection has benefitted greatly from the efforts of the anonymous reviewers who commented on earlier versions of the manuscript. Georgia Stewart, NAFSA's Director of Information Services, was instrumental in seeing the project through to fruition. Finally, this book would not have been completed without the valuable editorial assistance of Jennifer Love Costanza and computer consultation from Mike Bailey.

It is our hope that this collection will help staff members, faculty, and administrators of American universities develop locally viable solutions to the "foreign TA problem" in the spirit of international educational exchange.

Kathleen M. Bailey
Frank Pialorsi
Jean Zukowski/Faust

April 1984

# Foreword

Thirty years ago, I was a TA (teaching assistant). I had just returned from active duty with the U.S. Army in Korea, had just been admitted to graduate study after an absence of three years from any sort of serious intellectual endeavor, and had never taught in my life. I arrived on the campus no more than a week before classes started in September, was handed something labeled "Course Syllabus," together with a small packet of books (which the students shortly would be buying), was told to "read it all over," and—a few days later—was thrust into the classroom. I must confess that I was probably more frightened than I had ever been before. Had I read Bernard Malamud's *A New Life* then, I'm sure I could have seen the humor in my situation; not having read Malamud, I saw only the terror. I often have thought that the 35 freshmen entrusted to my tender mercies were cheated badly, and I have hoped that the remainder of their academic experience was better than was the portion I offered them.

Twenty years later, while working in India, I was invited to give a series of lectures at a private, parochial girl's college in a city in the south central part of the country. I agreed because the headmistress assured me that all the students spoke fluent English and because many of them were studying to be teachers of English, a field in which even now I believe I have some knowledge. I arrived to find the students jammed beyond capacity into a huge auditorium. It was a steamy day, and all the windows were flung wide open. The street noise was overwhelming. I started my lecture, mellifluously imparting wisdom in my northeastern American dialect, and was delighted to find the audience absolutely silent and attentive, smiling and nodding as I made each telling point. After talking for about an hour, I stopped and invited questions. There was a long silence. Presently a woman quite near the front raised her hand. When I recognized her, she stood, bowed politely, and said something. I had no idea what she said—I couldn't understand a word. She tried again and again, and in the end I had to ask the headmistress to "translate" for me. When the question finally penetrated, I realized that it was not at all related to anything I had said—the woman was interested to know whether I was married and, if so, how many children I had. There were, fortunately, only one or two other questions, all of which—though asked in English—had to be translated for me. At last, I escaped from the room and was accompanied back to my car by the headmistress. Realizing the scope of the communication problem, I asked her whether she thought the women had enjoyed my talk. She assured me that they had enjoyed it—after all, they had never before heard a native speaker of American English. But she did admit that it was unlikely that they had understood much. My pronunciation was, she said, so "unusual."

This book deals with something known as "The Foreign TA Problem." Indeed, as several of the authors point out, there is a problem. U.S. academic institutions are in the habit of using graduate students to teach entry-level courses. They do so because the labor is available and because the function provides a way to support graduate students. In the recent past, the number of non-native English speakers in the population of graduate students has increased—a phenomenon attributable to a variety of causes, both foreign and domestic, demographic and economic. This phenomenon has created a problem, but some aspects of the problem may have been blown out of proportion.

If my personal recollections are at all generalizable, the problem of being a TA is not a new problem. TAs have been sent forth without training for at least a couple of generations. The longevity of the practice is, of course, no justification for it. *All TAs ought to be trained before they begin to teach.* That is hardly a startling insight. After all, many of them plan to be college teachers, or will be forced into teaching because it is conventional for research scholars to justify their existence in this way. And if my Indian experience is generalizable, it is difficult to teach in a foreign environment even when the language is alleged to be the same.

Teaching is probably one of the most culture-sensitive activities, as anyone who has ever attempted to teach out of his or her culture well knows. This too is not a startling insight. The problem is not restricted to the inexperienced TA. There are, in U.S. colleges and universities, thousands of instructors with professorial rank who share in the problem because they are teaching out of their cultures and because English is not their native language. As some of the papers in this collection point out, the blame lies not only with the TA. He or she (though shes are relatively rarer) is the victim of the students' xenophobia and of the ethnocentricism of their parents. The TA suffers because it is unthinkable that the student/client might be wrong, because—unlike his professorial peer—he faces, Janus-like, in two directions, being neither truly student nor truly faculty, and therefore unprotected by academic tradition.

All this is not to deny that there is a problem. It is undeniable that some foreign TAs cannot operate in U.S. classrooms, cannot manage English adequately, and contribute more to confusion than to clarity. All of this is not to deny that the problem needs to be addressed. But at the same time, this is a plea to contemplate the issue in perspective. It is not only the foreign TA who may not know how to teach or how to communicate his meaning crisply, therefore let us not single him out for special censure. The problem needs attention, but attention should not become a license for a witch-hunt, as witch-hunts sometimes result in catastrophic solutions. Surely rational people who work in institutions predicated on rationality can approach the problem so as to perceive and treat all its causes. NAFSA is happy to contribute this volume as a bit of sanity in what rapidly is becoming a highly emotive environment. I trust that careful review of this material will lead to a more balanced resolution of the foreign TA problem.

Robert B. Kaplan
Los Angeles
NAFSA President, 1983-1984

# Part I
## *The Problem*

# The "Foreign TA Problem"[1]

## Kathleen M. Bailey

*U*. S. universities have long employed graduate students as teaching assistants to work as part-time instructors, test graders, discussion leaders, and laboratory session supervisors in classes for undergraduate students. In the past decade an increasing percentage of these teaching assistants (TAs) have been international students who are asssumed to be competent in their disciplines, but who have—to varying degrees—less than perfect control of English, the medium of instruction. Furthermore, these non-native speaking (NNS) TAs may lack a clear understanding of their roles within the American educational system. Thus both linguistic and cultural differences contribute to the difficulties faced by foreign TAs. Consequently, the interaction between non-native speaking teaching assistants and their students is complicated and sometimes problematic.

The communication difficulties engendered by this situation are collectively labeled the "foreign TA problem."[2] The purpose of this book is to address this problem, which should be viewed within the framework of two larger overlapping issues: the TA system as a whole and international educational exchange. This introductory chapter will discuss the context of the problem, including the role of TAs in U.S. universities, and the screening and training of international TAs. Since this book is intended to help college faculty and staff members deal with the so-called foreign TA problem, the various chapters will provide both practical advice and theoretical insights on these issues.

## Context of the Problem

Like most difficulties in human communication, the foreign TA problem is perceived and explained differently by the various people involved. The main participants are (1) the university faculty and administration, (2) the students, and their parents, and (3) the international TAs themselves.

## *The University's Perspective*

The point of view of many universities is summed up well in the following excerpts from a report written by a task force (Cole et al. n.d., 1-2) at the University of Alabama. Three important assumptions underlie the committee's position on the foreign TA problem:

> First, we place a high value upon having international students among our student body and upon having qualified international graduate asistants and professors assisting us in our on-going teaching, research, and service responsibilities. While these individuals certainly benefit from the education and employment they receive, their presence and active participation in the educational process also benefit our native students and the university.
>
> Second, we have realized that the situation regarding the English language proficiency and teaching ability of international graduate assistants is complex and not amenable to an immediate solution that will satisfy all concerned. We are dealing not only with individuals who may have already developed pronunciation patterns resistant to change, but also with individuals who come from cultures and educational systems that place different expectations for teaching methods and practices upon their participants.
>
> And third, U.S. students are a part of the problem which is extremely difficult to address. Research indicates that some U.S. students decide they will have difficulty understanding their instructor simply upon learning that the instructor is an international. This attitude can be changed very slowly, but only through U.S. students' increased contact with people from other countries in both educational and social settings.

The task force at the University of Alabama went on to recommend several steps for alleviating the foreign TA problem. These steps included increasing the applicant pool for teaching assistantships, adopting screening mechanisms for determining potential foreign TAs' English language skills, requiring attendance at a training program for all new foreign TAs, closer departmental supervision of foreign TAs, and establishing an intensive English language center at the university which would be responsible for training foreign TAs in the future.

## *The Students' and Parents' Perspective*

University administrators and faculty members have been pressed to deal with the foreign TA problem because of complaints from students about the oral English proficiency of foreign TAs. But, as was suggested by the University of Alabama's task force report, the students' ethnocentrism is sometimes part of the problem.

In dealing with this complex situation, administrators and faculty members must remember that undergraduate students, particularly freshmen and sophomores, occupy the lowest rungs on the academic ladder. In some ways they seem virtually powerless to affect the system that educates them. Yet they (and their parents) are also the consumers in this system, and as such they can easily tap into the philosophy that the customer is always right. Their instructional needs must be met if their tuition and their parents' tax dollars are to be judged well spent.

The usual forum for students' complaints has been the campus newspaper.

The following excerpt from a letter to the editor of the Minnesota Daily is typical:

> . . . It is not fair for students to take a class such as math, economics, or statistics, and listen to someone whom they cannot understand lecture, but whose material they are responsible for. . . . It is ridiculous to go in to obtain individualized instruction when students can't understand the teacher to begin with (cited in Mestenhauser et al. 1980, 3-4).

Similar problems have been noted in campus newspapers at the University of Pennsylvania (Shaw 1982), the University of Maryland (Kelley 1982), and UCLA (Swanbeck 1981; Timmerman 1981).

Unfortunately, the students' attitude is often justified. However, research by Orth (1983) at the University of Texas has shown that students' evaluations of foreign TAs correlate more strongly with a measure of their grade dissatisfaction than with their ratings of the TAs' English. This finding illustrates the complexity of dealing with students' perceptions of non-native speaking TAs.

For many college administrators, the foreign TA problem boils down to the fact that students' complaints are often followed by parents' complaints. Two examples of such letters are quoted here to illustrate the perspective of concerned parents. Both were written in May 1980, regarding teaching assistants at UCLA. The first was addressed to the governor of California:

> As one dedicated to assuring that the University of California system provides California citizens with quality education, you will undoubtedly wish to assist in initiating corrective action to remedy an existing problem in the instructional process. I refer to the current practice of employing foreign students as TEACHING ASSISTANTS (TAs).
>
> First, let me state that I believe that the TA is being utilized to the point where he is replacing the professor in many instances. Second, an ability to communicate clearly in the English language should be a mandatory requisite for receiving a TA assignment. Third, with the cost of college education rapidly growing beyond the financial means of many middle income parents, I believe TA assignments and all other campus jobs should be reserved for established California residents who need financial subsidy. (I understand it is a common practice at UCLA to provide a tuition waiver to foreign student TAs— who comprise a significant proportion of current TAs.)
>
> I have a young son who is a freshman at UCLA and who is having one "hell-of-a-time" as a result of an inability to obtain understandable help from his assigned TAs in calculus and chemistry. He has even changed classes in an attempt to improve the situation, only to find himself faced with another TA who is unintelligible. This is a totally unacceptable learning situation.
>
> I would appreciate your comments on this problem and your assistance in effecting a remedy. . . . As an overburdened taxpayer, I know of no good reason why I should be subsidizing the education of foreign students—send them home!

The second letter was addressed to the chancellor of the University with copies sent to California senators, congressmen, and assemblymen:

> It has been brought to my attention that many foreign students are employed as Teaching Assistants (TAs) at UCLA, many of whom are virtually inarticulate in English, and, thus, worse than ineffective in communicating with the students. Not only are they of no help, but cause confusion in the minds of those they are trying to teach. You and I well know that communication at best is often difficult, even among natives of the same language, specially as pertains to abstract ideas such as occur in philosophy, psychology, and the general subjects of the humanities.
>
> As a tax-paying Californian, I resent supporting a policy which dilutes the teaching

process by such an obvious abrogation of common sense; putting square pegs in round holes was never my idea of efficiency.

Additionally, if some of the TA appointments are to subsidize needy students, then all the more reason they should go to the sons and daughters of Californians, to wit, "Charity begins at home!" I am looking forward to some comments and/or explanation regarding the foregoing from your office.

As these letters reveal, the performance of non-native speaking teaching assistants has become an emotion-laden issue. Several factors which have contributed to this problem have been cited by researchers at the University of Minnesota. These factors include "an emerging 'new' ethnocentrism on the part of U.S. students" (and, one might add, parents), an "increasing attitude of consumerism among U.S. students" and "increasing demands for quality education and accountability" (Mestenhauser et al. 1980, 3).

A groundswell of such complaints from parents and undergraduates has prompted the recent efforts to upgrade the communication skills of NNS TAs at several colleges. Indeed, concern about the foreign TA problem is manifest in many sectors of the university community. Graduate divisions, academic departments, learning skills centers, TA training offices, departments of English as a second language (ESL), and foreign student advisers have all contributed to the activities described in this book.

## The Foreign TAs' Perspective

Survey research (Bailey 1982a) conducted at UCLA suggests that the "typical" foreign teaching assistant is a male pursuing a doctoral degree in math, engineering, or the sciences. There is about a one-in-three chance that he is Asian. In questionnaire data from eighty-one NNS TAs, three-fourths of the respondents reported having studied English for seven years or longer. Nearly a third of these TAs (32 percent) rated their spoken English as "fluent" while more than a third (39 percent) said theirs was "good" or "very good."

The respondents were also asked whether they thought foreign TAs should have to pass an oral English exam before being awarded teaching assistantships at UCLA. Half the respondents said they should not be required to take such an exam, while over a third felt they should. The remaining TAs said it depends on the discipline—that teaching some subjects requires greater English proficiency. In particular, they felt it was not necessary to speak English well in order to teach mathematics.

In addition, the TAs in this sample were asked to rate their own teaching performance. Three-fourths described their teaching as "good" or "very good." About equal proportions of TAs said their teaching had been either "excellent" or "fair." No one described his own teaching as "poor." However, there was only a low correlation ($r = .29$, $p<.05$) between these TAs' self-ratings and their students' evaluations of their teaching, which suggests that the NNS TAs and the students are not using the same criteria to judge the TAs' teaching success.

The questionnaire included an open-ended item which asked, "In your opinion what problems do non-native speaking TAs encounter with their American undergraduate students that native English speaking TAs don't (or probably don't) have?" While some TAs did not answer or said there were no problems, many listed more than one problem in answering this question. Among the difficulties most often cited (in descending order of frequency) were cultural differences between TAs and students, finding the right words to express one's ideas, students' complaints about the TAs' pronunciation, general communication problems, and a lack of trust from the students, who blame the TAs for their comprehension problems with the subject matter. This attitude was also expressed in follow-up interviews. Many of these subjects felt that their English problems provided American students, who were often described as "immature" or "lazy," with an easy excuse for their poor performance in class and on tests.

These comments illustrate the wide discrepancy between the students' perspective and the NNS TAs' perspective on the "foreign TA problem." The reality of the situation, if one reality can be isolated, probably lies somewhere in between these two extremes. In practice, it becomes the responsibility of faculty members and TA trainers to make sure that foreign TAs (1) have a clear understanding of their roles and responsibilities as TAs, and (2) speak English well enough to do their jobs.

## The Role of Teaching Assistants in American Universities

The question arises as to how the university can ensure that foreign TAs speak English well enough to convey the course material to their students. Another important question regards what sorts of cross-cultural communication and teaching skills a foreign TA must attain in order to do his job successfully.

However, these questions raise some debatable issues. How should oral English proficiency be assessed and quantified? What definition of success will be used and how will success be measured? According to whose perceptions should success and English proficiency be determined? What can universities do to improve foreign TAs' communicative competence? What can the TAs themselves do in this situation? What exactly is the role they are expected to perform?

Graduate students are employed as TAs at most large universities in the United States. Although teaching assistants may indeed assist professors in grading exams or preparing materials, they are often more directly involved in undergraduate instruction than their title would indicate. Many supervise laboratory experiments, lead discussion sections which complement professors' lectures, tutor students, hold office hours, and even teach independent courses.

This variability in the TAs' role contributes to the difficulty of describing what it means to be a successful TA.

Many people with very different perspectives have written about TAs' roles in contemporary American education. One undergraduate student has said that

> a TA is a kind of middle person in the educational institution. TAs lack the status of the faculty member, who engages primarily in research and teaching activity. TAs have previously, and very successfully, completed the activities in which the undergraduate is currently involved (Gurnick 1981, 3).

Gurnick also notes that undergraduates view the TA "as a sort of apprentice instructor, but as one whose function is to enhance their learning experience more so than to learn how to teach" (ibid.).

This dual role has also been discussed by Caramagno, who is himself an experienced teaching assistant. He has referred to TAs as "'academic hermaphrodites,' a species sporting parts of both academic sexes—students and faculty" (1981, 2). Another TA has said that "it is the half-way nature of the TA's position between students and professors which provides both unique teaching opportunities and potential headaches" (Lewthwaite 1981, 5).

Professors and administrators have also commented on the role of TAs. A decade ago a TA trainer wrote that

> teaching assistants perform several important functions at the university. Their responsiblity ranges from supervised, quasi-clerical assistance for a professor to completely autonomous instructional decision making for a large undergraduate class (Rose 1972, 102).

Apparently the situation has not changed much in the last ten years. A faculty member has recently asserted that the "role of the teaching assistant is mostly fortuitous, depending largely upon how each department or individual professor defines the position" (Von Blum 1981, 1).

As these comments reveal, both the TAs' role and individuals' expectations of that role may vary widely. But whatever the breadth of the position and the expectations may be, TAs are responsible for a substantial proportion of the undergraduate instruction in U.S. universities. However, in spite of this central role, relatively few TAs are recruited specifically for their teaching abilities or their interest in teaching careers. Instead, most schools use teaching assistantships as a way of "providing undergraduate instruction, and of providing financial support for graduate students, not as a means of training future college teachers" (Stockdale and Wochok 1974, 345).

In a scathing review of the TA system, Lnenicka claims that using TAs as anything other than assistants is detrimental to the education process:

> The undergraduate student and his parents, who suffer financial strain in order to provide for their children's college education, have a right to feel cheated and resentful when they find even one of the important courses in the undergraduate curriculum being taught by a graduate student, one who, in all probability, is inexperienced, unrehearsed, untrained for teaching, and whose primary interest lies not in teaching, but rather in satisfying the requirement for his own degree (Lnenicka 1972, 97).

Other academicians have shared Lnenicka's concern. Staton-Spicer and Nyquist report a trend of "growing concern about the improvement of the teaching effectiveness of graduate teaching assistants" (1979, 199). They state that teacher improvement (for both TAs and faculty members) has become an important issue in American education: "In the 1970s, programs began to emerge and, currently, something of a movement surrounds the improvement of teaching in higher education" (ibid., 200).

## Training Programs for Teaching Assistants

Indeed, the literature bears out this claim of increased attention to TA training in the 1970s. In fact, training programs for native-speaking TAs have been described for many disciplines, including business (Buckenmeyer 1972), chemistry (Barrus, Armstrong, Renfrew, and Garrard 1974; Siebring 1972), physics (Muhlestein and DeFacio 1974), speech/communications (Staton-Spicer and Nyquist 1979), economics (Lewis and Orvis 1973), English as a second language (Bailey and Campbell 1977), and foreign languages (Azevedo 1976; Goepper and Knorre 1980; Hagiwara 1976). Stockdale and Wochok (1974) have surveyed a number of subject-specific TA training programs offered at fifty different universities, but some schools also offer campuswide TA training programs. For example, Rose (1972) has described a program which stressed criterion-referenced instruction as a means of improving the teaching effectiveness of TAs across disciplines.

In the past decade there have been numerous attempts to upgrade the quality of instruction undergraduates receive from their TAs. However, as Siebring has pointed out,

> training programs of this type can succeed only when the quality of graduate students is such that they can benefit from such training. If graduate students are admitted *who lack proficiency with the English language* or have not mastered the undergraduate curriculum to a minimum level, the training sessions are not going to produce capable teaching assistants (1972, 99; emphasis added).

Thus the current efforts to deal with the "foreign TA problem" should be viewed in the wider context of the TA system and over a decade of efforts to upgrade TAs' teaching skills.

## Non-native Speaking Teaching Assistants

In 1976 researchers at the University of Minnesota reported an early finding on the limited English-speaking abilities of some NNS TAs (as perceived by students). Seven hundred undergraduates were surveyed for their ideas on improving TA effectiveness. At that time thirty of the respondents (4 percent) recommended means to "guarantee that foreign students hired as teaching assistants have sufficient mastery of the English language to insure effective communication with students" (Berdie, Anderson, Wenberg, and Price 1976, 171).

Three years after that study, as a result of complaints and letters to the editor of the campus newspaper, researchers at the same university conducted the International Issues Survey (cited in Mestenhauser et al. 1980). In a summary item about foreign TAs, more that 43 percent of the respondents said that a foreign TA had harmed course quality whereas only 9 percent indicated that a foreign TA had helped. Mestenhauser et al. concluded that "whether or not actual deficiencies existed among foreign TAs when compared to their U.S. counterparts, there was clearly a generalized perception that such was the case" (1980, 7). This survey was conducted in a situation where NNS TAs comprised approximately 24 percent of the total TA population, while the foreign students constituted only 17 percent of the total student population.

In a similar vein, one of the University of California student regents, commenting on the use of TAs in undergraduate instruction, has written that

> the system will never be any better than the TAs that comprise it. Some TAs have evoked criticism for not speaking English well enough to communicate with students in class. Obviously if this communication does not occur, the students are being hurt rather than assisted by the presence of the TA in the classroom (Lurie 1981, 4).

Thus these comments echo the survey results reported at the University of Minnesota (Mestenhauser et al. 1980, cited above), in which undergraduates perceived many foreign TAs as hindering rather than helping, the education process.

Furthermore, the topic of discussion apparently interacts with U.S. students' reactions to foreign TAs. In doctoral research conducted at the University of Minnesota, Keye (1981) found that freshman composition students rated foreign TAs' presentations on cultural topics more highly than their presentations on academic subject matter.

Concern for the English language abilities of foreign TAs has sparked the appearance of training programs at many colleges. These include the University of Southern California (Cheney-Rice, Garate, and Shaw 1980a and 1980b; Macer 1982; Shaw and Garate, this volume), Texas Tech (Smith 1982), Cornell University (Beukenkamp 1981), the University of Michigan (Ard and Rounds 1982), the University of Indiana (Friedman and Bier 1982), the University of Minnesota (Dege 1981; Keye 1981; Landa and Perry 1980 and this volume; Mestenhauser et al. 1980), the University of Houston (Acton 1980), Harvard (Sadow and Maxwell 1983), the University of Illinois at Champaign-Urbana (Berns, personal communication), the University of Pittsburgh (Cake and Menasche 1982), the University of Ohio (Heyde Parsons and Szelagowski 1983), and SUNY-Buffalo (Rice, this volume). Training programs for NNS TAs have been offered at five campuses of the University of California: UC Davis (Franck and DeSousa 1980), UC Irvine (Gaskill and Brinton, this volume), UC Berkeley (*San Francisco Examiner*, 1978), and UCLA (Hinofotis and Bailey 1978, 1980). Recently, a program was instituted in Taipei to help prepare graduate students as TAs before they arrive in this country (Young and Wang, 1982).

Turitz (this volume) has conducted survey research on several of these programs, which she classifies as short orientation-type programs given prior to the beginning of school or longer seminars offered during the college term. The chapters in this book which deal with particular programs are arranged according to Turitz's classification of orientation programs (Bailey and Hinofotis, Gaskill and Brinton, and Shaw and Garate) and seminar programs (Landa and Perry, Rice, and Zukowski/Faust).

In addition, the Foreign Student Adviser's Office at the University of Iowa has produced a helpful manual for foreign TAs (Althen 1981). It provides information about a variety of topics and sources of help.

Interest in the problems of non-native speaking TAs goes beyond the concerns of individual institutions, however. The National Association for Foreign Student Affairs (NAFSA) has recently named this issue as one of its priorities. In fact, NAFSA awarded a grant to the University of Minnesota to develop a series of videotapes for training international TAs and for providing guidance in establishing such training programs (see Mestenhauser et al. 1980). These videotapes may be borrowed by writing to NAFSA, while the manual which accompanies them may be purchased from the International Student Adviser's Office at the University of Minnesota.

Panel presentations on this topic have been held at several NAFSA conferences in the past five years and articles have appeared in the *NAFSA Newsletter* (Landa and Perry 1980; Heyde Parsons and Szelagowski 1983). Publication of this volume is yet another measure of NAFSA's concern about the foreign TA issue.

TESOL (Teachers of English to Speakers of Other Languages) and its affiliates have also taken a professional interest in this topic, since college administrators often turn to ESL departments for help with the foreign TA problem. This issue has been addressed in several TESOL conference presentations as well as in articles appearing in TESOL publications (e.g., Bailey 1983a; Friedman and Bier 1982; Hinofotis and Bailey 1980; Hinofotis, Bailey, and Stern 1981; Sadow and Maxwell 1983; Smith 1982).

## Problems in Screening NNS TAs

This review depicts a flurry of activity which is both widespread and recent. But what circumstances have led to this proliferation of ESL-based training programs for NNS TAs? Why are international graduate students not screened for English proficiency before they are awarded TA positions?

Most American universities do require scores on the Test of English as a Foreign Language (TOEFL) or some other standardized English test (e.g., the Michigan Test) as a prerequisite to admission. However, the TOEFL does not include a direct test of oral English proficiency; there is no subtest which involves an interview or the generation of spoken utterances by the test-taker. Nor can a speaker's degree of accentedness be measured by this "paper and pencil" test.

The use of TOEFL scores for screening NNS TAs is problematic, especially since Hinofotis (1976) found only a moderate correlation between foreign students' interview scores and their TOEFL scores ($r = .40$, $n = 52$) at Southern Illinois University. Higher correlations were found between the interview scores and the school's local placement examination ($r = .68$, $n = 106$). Hinofotis's findings have been corroborated by research conducted at Educational Testing Service (ETS), in which TOEFL scores correlated with scores from a direct oral proficiency measure, the Test of Spoken English, in the .56 to .71 range (Clark and Swinton 1980, 19).

As these moderate correlations reveal, written test scores are not necessarily good predictors of a candidate's oral proficiency. For this reason, graduate students exempt from required ESL courses by virtue of their scores on a written test may not be fluent speakers of English. Consequently, some graduate students who have done well on the TOEFL, but whose oral production skills may not be as good as their other English skills, have become teaching assistants at many U.S. universities.

In fact, the Test of Spoken English was developed by ETS because many academic and professional groups needed a reliable and economical way to measure oral proficiency. This tape-recorded test can be administered overseas, so some schools have begun to use it as an initial screening mechanism with foreign applicants for TAships. The chapter by Stansfield and Ballard (this volume) discusses the use of the Test of Spoken English (TSE) for this purpose.

Clark and Swinton (1980) have conducted research in which the TSE and the Foreign Service Institute (FSI) Oral Interview were both used to predict students' evaluations of foreign teaching assistants, as measured by the Student Instructional Report (SIR), a computerized questionnaire for the assessment of college teaching (Centra, 1980). The SIR includes supplemental items about the instructor's English which the students complete when the teacher being evaluated is not a native speaker. Clark and Swinton found low to moderate correlations between TSE scores and various categories of students' evaluations of non-native speaking TAs.

In a similar vein, Bailey (1982a) conducted research in which trained testers rated the English of foreign teaching assistants on the FSI Oral Interview. Students' assessment of their NNS TAs' oral communication skills (as measured by a modified version of the Student Instructional Report) were correlated with their evaluations of those TAs' teaching skills. Only moderate correlations obtained between the students' ratings of the TAs' teaching and the testers' ratings of their oral English *fluency*, one of the subscales of the FSI Oral Interview. (Interviews are scored on a scale of "0" to "5" with a "0" being no functional competence in the language and a "5" being the equivalent of an educated native speaker.) However, those TAs receiving a score lower than "2" on the FSI scale were judged by the students to be significantly different (i.e., worse) than NNS TAs rated as "2" or better by the professional testers.

Furthermore, those students who did *not* share a common major with their teaching assistants were found to be significantly more critical of NNS TAs than those students who did. This finding suggests that there is some validity to the foreign TAs' claim that students complain about their English out of resentment at having to take difficult required courses. It also suggests that some complaints from students might be avoided if NNS TAs were assigned to those classes designed for students majoring in the particular discipline.

Anecdotal evidence suggests that some academic departments consider test scores in determining NNS TAs' assignments. For example, foreign graduate students who have not been exempted from required ESL classes have sometimes been given test-grading responsibilities until they have completed those courses. In other cases, however, foreign graduate students who are not necessarily fluent speakers of English have been responsible for running laboratory sections, discussion groups, and tutorials. Their classroom performance has drawn criticism from some students, but this criticism is largely undocumented or unspecific. It may relate to purely linguistic factors, to teaching style, to a lack of experience, or to problems in cross-cultural communication.

Direct oral proficiency measures, such as the FSI Oral Interview and the Test of Spoken English, are certainly better screening mechanisms than are written exams. (See Stansfield and Ballard, this volume, for research evidence to support this claim.) However, faculty members and administrators must remember that non-native speaking TAs' oral English scores achieve only moderate correlations with their teaching evaluations. For this reason Bailey (in press) has argued in favor of local performance testing of foreign TA candidates in addition to initial oral proficiency testing.

In a performance test, the examinee must demonstrate his ability to use his English language skills in the same way they will be used on the job. In the case of foreign TAs, such a test might include a videotaped role play in which the candidate must explain subject-specific terms to a class of students, entertain questions, check the students' understanding of the concept, deal with an interruption, make a homework assignment, and end the lesson (ibid.). A panel composed of faculty members, experienced TAs, and undergraduate students could then rate the candidate's performance.

## Concluding Remarks

The graduate division dean or departmental chairperson who has read this far may wonder whether the foreign TA problem is not best dealt with by circumvention: one could avoid it by not awarding teaching assistantships to foreign students. But this seeming solution is both unrealistic and unfair, and in the long run it would work to the detriment of American undergraduates as well as foreign graduate students.

TA selection committees are well aware that the pool of native English speaking TA applicants, particularly in engineering, math, and the sciences, has grown or shrunk in response to economic forces outside the university community. In the absence of qualified native speaking applicants for TAships, academic departments that do not wish to hire NNS TAs are faced with two options: (1) hiring unqualified native speakers, or (2) allowing the ratio of undergraduate students to professors and/or TAs to increase, thereby almost certainly limiting students' access to the instructional staff. Of course, neither of these options is acceptable. They would both directly harm the quality of undergraduate instruction.

Foreign graduate students who work as international TAs can contribute a great deal to U.S. universities. These young scholars are typically among the brightest and most promising professionals at their home universities. They come to our colleges with educational experiences different from those of their American peers. They probably also bring different world views, which can broaden the scope of their undergraduate students considerably—provided the channels of communication are open.

As these foreign graduates return to their home countries, having completed master's or doctoral degrees at U.S. institutions, they will assume positions of authority in colleges, industry, and government. One feels compelled to remind the disgruntled taxpaying parents whose letters were quoted above that the U.S. is likely to fare better in international relations if at least some of the leaders of other nations' business and civic affairs have been influenced by positive international educational exchanges in this country. (Of course, if a foreign graduate student's teaching experience is disastrous, it is unlikely to be a source of positive attitudes.)

The foreign TA problem, then, is related to all the following interacting variables:

1. Teaching assistants are responsible for a great deal of undergraduate instruction in varying capacities, even though they may not be highly experienced or highly motivated as teachers.
2. The 1970s witnessed an increased emphasis on TA training and on instructional accountability in American higher education, which contributed to an attitude of consumerism among undergraduate students and their parents.
3. Relative to the number of foreign graduate students particularly in math, engineering, and the sciences, declining proportions of American students in graduate schools have made foreign TAs more numerous and more visible.

4. Undergraduate students, while often having valid reasons to complain, sometimes respond to their non-native speaking TAs' foreignness with an attitude of annoyed ethnocentricism.

5. International educational exchanges, including the awarding of TAships to qualified foreign graduate students, are desirable in terms of tangible present-day rewards and less obvious long-term results.

All of these factors suggest that proposed solutions to the foreign TA problem must go beyond accent improvement and English language training. Consequently, a number of ESL-based programs developed for foreign TAs have also offered instruction in teaching techniques, communication strategies, public speaking, and nonverbal communication. The chapters by Gaskill and Brinton, Landa and Perry, Rice, and Zukowski/Faust explain how this diverse course content is covered in various programs.

The chapters in this collection have been chosen to convey a variety of institutional responses to the foreign TA problem. They reflect NAFSA's commitment to ongoing international educational exchange. It is the authors' hope that the ideas presented here will help U.S. universities effect locally viable solutions to this complicated situation.

## Endnotes

1. This chapter is based on portions of the author's doctoral dissertation (Applied Linguistics, UCLA). For more information see Bailey (1982a). Earlier versions of this paper benefited from the constructive criticism of Russ Campbell, Frances Hinofotis, Harold Levine, and Georgia Stewart.

2. The "foreign TA problem" is really something of a misnomer, since some foreign TAs are native speakers of English—whether from the United Kingdom, New Zealand, Canada, Australia, or other countries. Therefore, although several chapters in the collection refer to "foreign TAs" or "international TAs," the phrase "non-native speaking TAs" is perhaps more accurate. However, throughout this book, these terms will be used interchangeably.

# Toward an Anthropology of the Classroom: An Essay on Foreign Teaching Assistants and U.S. Students

## FRANK PIALORSI

Sometimes, as with Isaac Newton and the apple, it pays to take a closer look at what so many consider the obvious and especially at what is obvious about ourselves. The attempt here is to juxtapose universals of culture and specific American cultural traits in order to provide insight into the behavior of our young people, especially in the classroom setting, and to show teachers, administrators, and TA trainers why some of this conduct may be problematic to the uninitiated foreign teaching assistant.

This chapter is intended to describe the relationship of education to society as well as the participants' roles in the education process. The title is derived from Sol Tax's definition of anthropology as "an association of people who have agreed to continue in communication with each other" (cited in Hymes 1972, 7). By definition, at least for the duration of their professional relationship to one another, U.S. students and foreign teaching assistants must agree to communicate.

In a continuing commitment to international education, U.S. universities have paid increasing attention to the roles and varying performances of the foreign TAs they employ. These men and women, because of their impressive academic backgrounds at home, have been selected by graduate committees to instruct American undergraduates in fields ranging from linguistics to watershed management. One of the more positive aspects of these appointments is that the foreign TA often presents a different view and interpretation of the course material, and takes an approach to the subject that U.S. academicians may not have considered. And, in the long run, such a professional arrangement provides the opportunity for international cross-communication among future political, scientific, and academic leaders.

Some specific notable negative aspects have also surfaced. First, variation in the use of English among foreign TAs interferes with student comprehension. Problems such as a foreign accent and non-native syntax are confusing to American students. Second, a lack of understanding by the foreign TA of the diversified U.S. education system or an unclear picture of the "anthropology" of the U.S. university classroom prevents effective teaching and learning. And finally, a conflict of educational values between cultures often emerges.

The foreign TA, like any foreign student coming to study at an American university, must undergo a process of acculturation in order to be effective in the U.S. classroom. In other words, he or she must, to an as yet undetermined degree, "become more like us" in order to function.

The most obvious manifestation of the acculturation process is learning the target language. Cautious linguists question a remark such as "Jane is fluent in five languages." To be truly fluent in a language, in addition to mastering the phonology, morphology, syntax, and even the semiology of that language, Jane must become aware of its other aspects, such as the variations of idiolect—the language behavior of an individual speaker—a task that causes agonies of misunderstanding even among native speakers. She must be aware of social stratification within certain language groups, as well as appropriate levels of formality to suit the event or topic.

Much of the data on foreign TAs and their students indicate that both groups place great emphasis on the language problem, especially pronunciation, without putting it in the totality of culture; however, many a non-native speaker who "massacres" English, is still able to get his message across with just the proper amount of candor, humor, or poignancy, because he has mastered other characteristics of the language and culture such as timing and jargon. Perhaps most important, the listeners sense the acculturated non-native speaker's insight into their view of the world and their place in it.

When the foreign TA is introduced to the important concept of culture and the need to examine it, he or she finds that education, formal and informal, is part of every culture. The task lies in identifying prominent universals.

At this point, we should develop a working definition of culture. There are many such definitions, a few hundred in fact. E.B. Tylor's, for example, might effectively describe the range of variables a foreigner in a new culture must confront:

> Culture is that . . . complex whole which includes knowledge, beliefs, art, morals, law, custom, and any other capabilities and habits acquired by man as a member of society (1972).

Another definition that is especially suitable for foreign TAs attempting to get along with their American students is Keesing's statement that "culture is the totality of learned, socially transmitted behavior" (1958, 30).

With either of these definitions in mind, the foreign TA should consider the necessity for a switching of cultural roles along with the switching of languages for successful teaching in a foreign university. The ability to assume a culturally alien persona is an important part of what we mean by capacity for language or overall communicative competence. Like an actor the foreign TA must assume the role of teacher.

One characteristic of education is its relationship to the social power base. According to Kneller (1965, 66), the dominant group in a culture organizes the system of education to maintain and strengthen its own position. Of course, this power structure has been challenged many times, as in the 1960s when the students, the educated elite, rebelled against "the system" in several countries.

A second characteristic of education is that all cultures use rewards and punishments to encourage learning and to correct aberrant behavior. The United States, throughout its educational history, has been extreme in its use of one or both of these devices at one time or another. But the subtle types of rewards and punishment used by adults or near-adults in unequal power discourse situations, such as the college classroom, may differ widely from culture to culture. Foreign TAs need to be aware that American students may expect praise for correct answers and resent negative feedback that seems to them too strong.

A third notable characteristic is that in all societies, educators of every nationality, intentionally or unintentionally, withhold crucial knowledge from children, young people, and the uninitiated adult learner. Foreign TAs should know that, in this society, such information may include facts about sex or transgressions of historical figures.

Finally, and probably the greatest problem in education in every country, is the challenge of dealing and cooperating intelligently with the inevitable sociocultural changes taking place. Educators continue to argue about whether or not we can or should actually use education to influence or control these changes. In the United States, our educators are expected to be seekers and explorers of knowledge, leaders in formulating the values and ideals of our society and in working for its continual improvement. An important cross-cultural question will be whether or not the foreign TA, on becoming a participant in the process of American higher education, can assume this role.

As for differences among cultures, these are too numerous for listing. American culture, for example, is much less integrated than, say, that of the Soviet Union, where the needs of farming and industry are an integral part of the educational foci. We can compare the blurred lines between childrearing at home and educating at school that exist in the United States to the strict compartmentalization of education in France and Germany. As Metraux has pointed out (1963, 125), because of the clear division of their responsibilities, there is little need for communication between parents and teachers or social leaders and teachers in those two European countries.

In the U.S., on the other hand, a trend of cooperation has developed between the school and the home (e.g., the very existence of the P.T.A.), and the school and other social institutions. At the same time we must remember that more than anywhere else in the world, universities here have traditionally reflected the social pluralism of our twentieth century and have provided the means for upward social mobility.

After developing an awareness of cultural differences and universals the foreigner should become familiar with the conflicts within a given culture. Nowhere is culture-in-conflict more obvious than in the United States, where opposing values coexist to a bewildering degree in the eyes of the foreigner, especially one from a tightly structured society such as Japan or China, or even West Germany. (This same bewilderment is also faced by the native American Indian who leaves the reservation to study at a southwestern university.) A broad example of conflicting values comes from Kneller:

> Consider the value of competitiveness. . . . Americans are constantly urged to get ahead; our aim is always to win, always to get there first, always to climb one more rung on an endless ladder of prosperity and success. . . . The American is . . . also pulled by contrary values, such as that of group harmony and cooperation (1965, 115).

The conflicting values of cooperation and competition are often painfully obvious in college classrooms, especially during discussions of test grades, lab report scores, and cheating.

Let us focus on classroom behavior specifically to demonstrate the conflict between the expectations of teachers and the norms of behavior. It is important for the foreign TA to know that U.S. students have been told over and over to be punctual or to be quiet when the teacher is talking. Since their elementary school years, American students have been asked to raise their hands to signal that they wished to speak or answer questions. In sports and games they learned to play fair and to take turns; they also developed a strong sense of group loyalty. However, as Kneller concludes, there has been no guarantee that the students ever absorbed these values as their own:

> . . . other factors interfere, such as the special norms of the peer group, the unpopularity of certain teachers, and perhaps parental apathy toward . . . education (ibid., 119).

In class, students at all grade levels often speak out without being called on or raising their hands. Jules Henry has described this permissiveness in its extremity:

> The excessive informality of . . . American schools stems from the teacher's deliberate refusal to establish a clear source of authority in the classroom, so that the children are often unsure where to draw the line in their behavior and whom precisely to heed, whether the teacher or one of their own number (1960, 285-286).

In college classrooms, although the lecture format is common, this tendency toward permissiveness often results in an interactive dialogue between students and professors, either during or after the professor's presentation.

American students today do differ from past generations in some ways. Their manners and mores have been shaped steadily by the experiences and fast-changing life-styles of their parents and daily by the influences of their peer groups, among whom a noticeable characteristic is in the choice of language style. What were outrageous obscenities rarely heard in mixed company twenty years ago, are now commonly heard qualifiers, part of the informal and, more and more, of the formal speech habits of both sexes, however blunted these phrases are by overuse. Non-native speaking teaching assistants, whose English instruction in their home countries probably did not include profanity, may be puzzled or offended by their students' speech.

Most likely, the foreign TA will be surprised by much of the behavior of the freshman undergraduates he encounters in his first teaching assignment. It behooves us to attempt a further profile of the kind of student he might expect to face in the classroom. Coming from the public high schools, students are accustomed to teachers who have lost or given up a great deal of authority in the classroom. Ideally, this loss of authority has been balanced by a kind of teamwork for problem solving—a partnership between students and teacher. However, critics of contemporary education, (e.g., Henry 1960) exhort the teacher to assume once again the authoritarian role of instructor and insist that the boundaries of social distance be re-examined. Today, in many classroom situations students are permitted to call teachers by their first names. This practice, of course, is more common at the graduate school level, but it may be surprising to foreign TAs from relatively formal educational backgrounds. In addition, college teachers here are usually expected to be approachable both in and out of the classroom.

Experience tells us that the class master, foreign or American, must maintain a delicate balance of discipline and permissiveness. If the instructor cannot lead, the students, even those used to a higher degree of permissiveness, become confused and anarchy results. On the other hand, if the instructor is excessively autocratic, the students are likely to become resentful and attempt to frustrate him.

What happens then in the university classroom? Because there is more at stake professionally and financially, the professor does wield more power than the typical high school teacher, in that the students' academic records have a greater impact on their future careers. Not since they were read to by their parents in their preschool days, do students in classrooms strive again to listen so carefully. In the lecture hall system, the social distance is wider between lecturer and students, but considerably less than when their parents attended college.

In summary, recognizing that students' educational backgrounds are in some ways similar but in many ways different should facilitate the foreign TAs' efforts to communicate with and understand their U.S. students. Most important, since this country has no national ministry of education, each community's school district and, in fact, each school has a style or character in some ways different from any other. Although the media have created a great deal of homogeneity nationwide, in each U.S. school setting one will find unique approaches to teaching and learning along with individual definitions of the student and teacher roles. The foreign TA must be aware of the great variety and elasticity of the American value system, thereby becoming more conscious of and sensitive to the expectations that students bring to the university classroom or lecture hall.

# Linguistic Competence, Communicative Needs, and University Pedagogy: Toward a Framework for TA Training[1]

PETER A. SHAW
ELENA M. GARATE

*T*his is a chapter which is more general than specific. It considers the problem of designing a course for the orientation and training of international teaching assistants in an American university. Explanatory and illustrative details are drawn from the authors' experience in such a course at the University of Southern California (USC).

This course is held in the month of August prior to the beginning of the fall semester. The program is intensive, with thirty-six hours a week of classroom activity accompanied by practical and cultural activities such as getting to know the university and its surrounding neighborhood and becoming familiar with the life and culture of Los Angeles. Instruction emphasizes language (pronunciation, fluency, communicative competence), culture (American undergraduate student behavior, the system of higher education in the United States), and pedagogy (course and lesson planning, classroom management skills).

## Linguistic and Communicative Competence

It will be argued here that a training course for international teaching assistants is an instance of an ESP program: English for specific purposes. One of the suppositions behind this view is the hope that the trainees arrive with a good command of the grammatical, lexical, and semantic systems of the language. That is, they have a general competence in the language. This, in fact, has been the experience at USC: almost without exception, trainees pass the

English placement test, which is given to all entering international students, and they require no further ESL training as students. However, even that statement is a little misleading: the same test is used for all students and is therefore, of necessity, a general test; the most realistic claim should be that the trainee's general proficiency in English determines that no further ESL training is required; his competence in English as a student of, say, physics, or as a teacher of physics has not been assessed.

One can go further in some cases and add that trainees often have a general communicative competence in that they can get along with native speakers in most social situations and certain more specialized situations. If, therefore, the TA trainee is a limited speaker of English, beginning or intermediate ESL student, then a different kind of course must be envisaged.

The general approach discussed here is based on the broad goals laid out in Figure 1. The term *language skills* here is equated with the ability to express meanings; the TA trainee arrives with a general ability to say what he means. The course will focus on his ability to express meanings in the content area he will be dealing with. This is contrasted with what has to be done with the language (communicative skills): managing the classroom, counseling students, establishing an appropriate relationship, giving feedback, and communicating information.

## Expressing Meanings

This distinction may be expressed in the framework developed by Wilkins (1977) and elaborated by van Ek (1976), Munby (1978), and others. Expressing meanings involves concepts: the propositional content of what we have to say. These meanings are sometimes referred to as ideational. Wilkins (1977) breaks down this aspect of meaning in his semantico-grammatical categories, which cover our perception of events, processes, states, and abstractions. These meanings are expressed through the grammatical system of English (hence the name of the categories). In attempting to convey our ideas, we select the appropriate form. The semantico-grammatical categories include time, quantity, space, relational meaning, and deixis. Each category is further subdivided. Space, for example, is broken down into dimensions, location and motion; quantity into divided and undivided reference, numerals, and operations.

Thus, when a math TA fails to properly express the derivation of an equation, or a physics TA cannot put into words the workings of a machine, or an economics TA confuses the sequence of events, it is the semantico-grammatical system which is breaking down. The fault, and the repair, will commonly be at the sentence level or below: lexical choice to express multiplication; the correct preposition to relate one part of the machine to another; the appropriate time expressions for sequencing events.

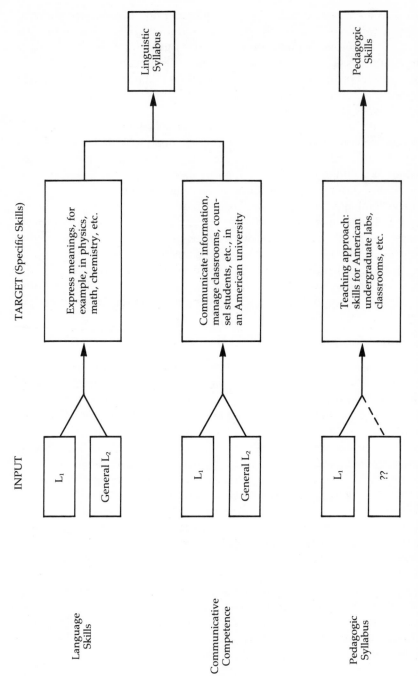

Figure 1. *General second language (L₂) skills, supported initially by first language (L₁) skills, become specific second language skills for international teaching assistants.*

## Communicative Functions

The use to which language is put leads away from the consideration of words, phrases, and sentences to a discussion of discourse. Sentences are put together to perform a particular function (although, as we shall see below, certain functions—defining, for example—may be expressed by a single sentence). These functions are classified by Wilkins into the categories of communicative function. They include judgment and evaluation, persuasion, argument, rational inquiry and exposition, personal emotions, and emotional relations.

It can now be seen how the two systems (the semantico-grammatical categories and the categories of communicative function) come together in the use of language. One cannot *suggest* without suggesting something: a function needs ideational content. Similarly, an action without some functional marker is not a suggestion. The function may be overt, as when a TA says, "I suggest we look at another example," or less explicit, as in "Why don't we look at another example?" or implied, as in "I wonder whether another example might not make it clearer." These are instances where function and form have a reasonably clear relationship: one sentence to one function, one function to one sentence. However, this is not always the case. One sentence may express more than one function; one function may be realized over a stretch of discourse.

Instances of the latter can be found in the category of rational inquiry and exposition, which includes:

> implication, deduction, supposition, conjecture, assumption, proposition, hypothesis, substantiation, verification, justification, proof, conclusion, demonstration, condition, consequence, result, inference, illustration, corollary, presupposition, interpretation, explanation, definition, exemplification, concession, purpose, cause, reason, classification, comparison, contrast, (and) generalization (Wilkins 1977, 53).

While some of these items will be localized in the discourse (giving an example or stating a presupposition), others will be realized over a considerable stretch (giving a classification, presenting a hypothesis). Thus, as suggested above, certain such functions—definition again being the best example—can be expressed in a single sentence ("The *atomicity* of an element is the number of atoms contained in one molecule of the element"), but most will involve a stretch of discourse. Again, classifying would be an example.

When an international TA develops a function over an extended stretch of language, breakdowns which take place may be much harder to prescribe and treat. Not the use of one word or phrase, not the construction of a particular sentence, but the whole design of the discourse may be at fault. This point will have interesting consequences for the design of a TA training course.

In summary, then, the language syllabus for the course will have two components, ideational meanings and functions, each appearing in a number of speech situations (see Figure 2). Although all situations will be covered, the presentation of information will obviously receive the greatest attention.

| SITUATIONS | IDEATIONAL MEANINGS | FUNCTIONS |
|---|---|---|
| Classroom management | the language of the college classroom and course, e.g., 'mid-term,' 'audit,' etc. | e.g., initiating the lesson |
| Organization of learning | | e.g., giving instructions |
| Classroom discourse | | |
| Lectures | the language of the discipline (physics, economics) plus the language used to express examples relevant to the students | e.g., defining, classifying, explaining |
| Review sessions | | e.g., clarifying |
| Discussions | | e.g., assigning turns |
| Question and answer sessions | | e.g., asking for clarification |
| Individual counseling | the language of counselling | e.g., offering alternatives |

Figure 2.  Components of a language syllabus for non-native speaking teaching assistants

## Communication Across Cultures

Finally, having analyzed the notion of communicative competence to some extent, we must examine the issue of communication across cultures. The crucial question concerns the means by which adequate communication with native speakers of another language is achieved (the ends of such communication having been roughly specified above in Figure 2). The situation here can be made to look very unpromising, given the problems depicted in Figure 3: The mismatch underlying the situation can be expressed in three equations:

1. in general, the TA's expectations of what happens in a university classroom do not match those of the students;
2. in particular, the TA's imported standards, that is what he thinks he can expect from the students, do not match the students' capabilities;
3. in particular, the students' standards, that is what they think they can expect from the TA, do not match the TA's capabilities.

These equations can be exemplified as follows.

First, in the TA's home situation, college students probably do not interrupt or ask questions during a lecture; in fact, to do so might lead to loss of face, as indications of lack of comprehension are a sign of weakness which is not normally displayed. The American student, on the other hand, is used to a situation where requests for clarification, repetition, and so on are quite common and where questions by students are welcomed. When the international TA first encounters this practice, the interruptions may be misinterpreted (as disruptive, hostile, or disrespectful), while the students may not understand his inability and apparent unwillingness to deal with their questions. This kind of mismatch in expectations can lead to severe breakdowns in communication.

Second, a physics or an economics TA may be entirely unprepared for the students' low level of ability in mathematics. He makes assumptions about the students' prior knowledge based on what students can do in his own country and, as a result, students cannot follow the lecture.

Finally, students come to expect a procedure in which a concept, while receiving a formal definition (often dictated or written on the blackboard), is further illuminated with informal restatements and illustrations related to their own culture and interests. When some or all these elements are lacking in presentations by international TAs, the students express difficulty in following and understanding the lesson.

Can the skills needed for adequate communication with the native speakers of another language be taught? One answer is given by Gumperz, Jupp, and Roberts (1979) in an introductory pamphlet that accompanies the BBC film "Crosstalk," which deals with issues of cross-cultural communication:

> A basic principle is that individuals cannot be taught to communicate effectively across cultures; it is something that they must learn for themselves. There is no single method which people can acquire and no set of rules which they can simply put into practice . . .

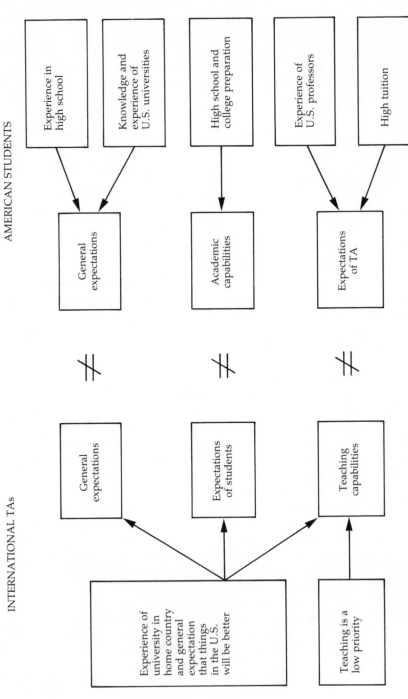

Figure 3. *Three unbalanced equations in the relationships of U.S. students and international TAs.*

because the way language is used has to take account of so many variables. Every piece of good communication depends on the response and feedback which participants expect from each other and every user of the language has to develop his own strategies for interpreting and responding appropriately.

From this, it is a short and obvious step to the principle (which is pursued here) that an ESP course must be built around a central core of activity in which the second language learner actually performs the tasks associated with his specific purpose, either in a real or a simulated context. In this case, the trainee must teach. The implications of this idea are pursued below.

This is not to suggest, of course, that the TA trainee's expectations and capabilities will not receive attention. In the former, information about the target culture as a whole and, specifically, the system of education must be forthcoming. In the latter, discussion of practice in planning, evaluation, materials preparation, and so on must be provided.

## ESP: English for Specific Purposes

It was claimed earlier that an international TA training course is a case of an ESP program, and some of the features of such a program were mentioned. This section deals with the issue of planning and executing such a course. These steps involve a general consideration of needs analysis and program development (although examples will be drawn from TA training).

Mackay and Bosquet (1981) suggest three broad stages: (1) the pre-program development stage, (2) the program development stage, and (3) the stage of program maintenance—a quality control stage. The pre-program development stage is characterized as a period of consultation and decision making. Typically, a problem is isolated and a commitment is made to take action to remedy the situation. The outcome is an expression of that commitment in the form of a rationale and the disssemination of that rationale to all the parties concerned. The details of this phase will generally be the same in any university situation: the increasing number of international TAs together with pressure from complaining students and concerned faculty will cause deliberations to begin over what action to take.

The program development stage is broken down into a number of phases. The first is an information-gathering phase, when interviews are conducted, questionnaires distributed, and classes are visited. This process provides the necessary information for the second phase: the specification of goals. Once realistic objectives have been set, the production phase can be initiated. This procedure involves the selection of language items, pedagogic activities, and other materials that will form the syllabus. Once assembled, these are broken down into teaching units, and appropriate classroom procedures to implement them are established.

These steps lead to a teacher training phase, which in this case was especially interesting as it largely consisted of establishing a dialogue between experienced ESL teachers who needed to know something about educational theory and practice in general and college-level pedagogy in particular, and experienced educators who were interested in knowing about the language and communication problems anticipated in the trainees. It should be stressed, perhaps, that the program designed in the process was never envisaged as the simultaneous implementation of two separate courses: an advanced ESL class and a teacher training course. On the contrary, the course design was intended to integrate the two foci as fully as possible.

One of the consequences of this decision can be seen in the production phase. The use of conventional ESL materials and textbooks was precluded by the decision to integrate the course as fully as possible. Thus it was necessary to find as many relevant samples of language in use as possible and to devise worksheets and other materials to accompany them. Much of the input material for the course therefore consisted of videotapes and films of teaching, counseling, and other aspects of the trainees' target activity. Where gaps in the available materials were identified, live demonstrations by the trainers were planned.

The final phase of the program development stage is the trial phase. Mackay and Bosquet (1981) recommend that materials be taught under such conditions that their effectiveness can be determined and changes made. While this process was attempted as an on-going activity during the course, the nature of our program (an intensive one-month assault) made this sort of evaluation very difficult to implement. Instead, the materials and activities are assessed in detail by all concerned at the end of the course and modifications are carried out before the following session begins. For this reason, the trial phase in this program coincided with stage three—the quality control stage—and cannot be considered a separate exercise.

In the same way, to return to the information-gathering phase, it is difficult to incorporate the trainees' own desires and perceived needs except in an ad hoc way. The trainees enter the country as little as 24 hours before the course begins; needs are therefore assessed on the basis of information gleaned from international TAs already here. Thus, where Mackay and Bosquet distinguish between four kinds of needs (future hypothetical needs, teacher-created needs, student desires, and real, current needs), a course such as ours must estimate what the real current needs will be and supplement them wherever possible with the students' (i.e., the foreign TAs') desires.

The work of Mackay and Bosquet draws on that of Munby (1978), whose Communicative Needs Processor is the most ambitious and detailed needs assessment instrument available. It is presented here, not as a model to be followed, but to underline some of the points made in the introduction as to what possible components should at least be considered in a needs analysis.

Munby's Communicative Needs Processor has nine parameters, each of which raises questions to be answered in determining the objectives of a training program:

1. The participant: what relevant information can be gained about the trainee? In this case, what is his mother tongue, country of origin, field of study, etc.?

2. Purposive domain: what content will be taught and what kind of teaching (lecture, lab, etc.) and other activities (e.g., counseling) are involved?

3. Setting: will teaching occur in a classroom, a lab, an amphitheater, an office, or the campus in general?

4. Interaction: what are the students like and how will they expect to interact with the TA?

5. Instrumentality: What medium is used (spoken or written) and in what mode and channel (lecture or discussive or interactive mode; face-to-face channel)?

6. Dialect: what are the characteristics of standard American academic dialect?

7. Target level: how clear, fluent, and error-free must the trainees' speech be?

8. Communicative event: can the functions involved be specified and matched with the subject matter?

9. Communicative key: how formal or informal, serious or frivolous, etc., should the trainee be?

This is not the place for a detailed consideration of these parameters. Clearly, they constitute a formidable battery for establishing objectives. They are raised here as issues to be addressed in designing a training program for foreign TAs.

In the next section, we turn to the issue of classroom activities and, in particular, to the setting up of a cycle of events which will attack the problem of training someone to communicate more effectively across cultures. Again, the point is repeated that this is not a question of selecting suitable materials or a textbook; it is a question of establishing and following certain procedures. Such procedures can lead to successful communication.

## Three Steps to Successful Communication

The three steps to successful communication proposed by Gumperz (e.g., in Gumperz, Jupp, and Roberts, 1979) are perception, acceptance, and repair. All three are necessary conditions to successful communication and none is sufficient by itself. While all are by no means easy, different TAs have problems with different steps, as the work of Landa and Perry (this volume) at Minnesota has shown. Certain trainees— fortunately, they seem to be a small minority— never achieve the first step. In other words, they never see that there is not complete understanding on both sides. Gumperz's model would predict that such trainees will not make noticeable improvements in their teaching and will take the first opportunity to leave teaching (becoming research assistants or the like) having had an uncomfortable experience in the classroom.

Others achieve the first step, but do not accept any responsibility for communication breakdown, blaming the students for lack of attention, lack of intelligence, or insufficient background knowledge of the subject. Again, the model predicts an uncomfortable, relatively unsuccessful, and often short-lived career for such TA trainees.

Most trainees achieve the first two steps, however. The most successful, we predict, are those who can take the third step and modify their behavior according to feedback and advice from trainers and students. However, such responses to the trainee are of little value unless he or she is open to advice because the first two steps have been achieved. We now examine these three steps in more detail.

## Perception

This stage involves a statement from the trainee to the effect that:

> I can see that the communication involving me and this group of students has not been entirely successful.

Repetitions of this experience then lead to a general perception:

> My attempts to communicate with American students in the classroom are not always successful.[2]

This step can be achieved in various ways, which arise from the central component of the USC course, a sequence of teaching assignments in which trainees receive immediate feedback from the audience (American undergraduates) and delayed feedback by reviewing a videotape of their teaching with an instructor. The first possibility is that the trainee realizes from the behavior of the students in class during a teaching assignment that communication is breaking down. This is most likely to happen if the students are participating to a noticeable degree. The second possibility arises during the feedback session immediately following the teaching assignment; it involves the students explaining what they did not understand and the trainee perceiving that the communication was, to some degree, unsuccessful. The third possibility comes in reviewing the videotape as the trainer draws the trainee's attention to points in the tape where communication broke down and the trainee recognizes that that was, in fact, the case.

We would predict that, initially, the latter two possibilities are more likely than the first. However, for a trainee who achieves the perception step early in the course by the first method, we would predict a rapid advancement in communication and pedagogic skills and a good chance of success as a TA. The second and third in combination are often a powerful means of effecting the perception step: that is, the trainee is dubious about the students' claims not to have understood but can later be shown evidence in the videotape of exactly how and why the breakdown took place. The combination of all three types of realization, though extremely rare because of some trainees' unwillingness to allow students to participate in the class, is clearly the most effective break-through.

## Acceptance

This process involves a statement from a trainee to the effect that:

A breakdown in communication has occurred between the students and myself. I accept that fact and I further accept that a deficiency or deficiencies in my communication skills brought about the breakdown.

Repetitions of the experiences of Perception and Acceptance in individual instances leads to a general Acceptance to the effect that

Unless I improve my communication skills, communication breakdown will continue to occur in my classes.

The second step thus makes way for the third. However, the implications of acceptance will not have escaped the reader. It is not easy for a mature individual who has considerable knowledge and expertise in his field and who may have been a respected teacher in his own country to acknowledge such a gap in his professional capabilities. This step suggests confrontation, conflict, and loss of face. One clearly does not want to urge TA trainees to such lengths unless they are necessary; but necessary is what we consider them to be.

It is not sufficient simply to inform international TAs that American students and American universities are different from those they encountered in their own country. They must find out for themselves; perhaps the biggest strength of the kind of course advocated here is that the confrontation necessary to effect the acceptance step is allowed to happen in the course, where it can be carefully monitored and contained, rather than in the real world. For in the real world, as we know, such confrontations can lead to complaints, poor evaluations, feelings of resentment and even, occasionally, to entire classes arriving in the department office to complain. The acceptance step is often a shock and many international TAs resist it for a considerable period of time. Yet, as mentioned above, we predict much greater success for those who make it, and especially for those who make it early.

## Repair

The repair step essentially involves five elements. In the first, the TA asks for and is supplied with relevant information about the background, nature, expectations, and skill levels of American students as well as information about the high school and college educational system. Activities range from talks, lectures and discussions, simulations, films, exhibits (from high school year-books to student newspapers), to visits and contact with American students. Second, the TA asks for and is supplied with relevant information about the cultural background of the situation he will have to deal with: the general culture of the area (in this case, Los Angeles and Southern California) and the subculture of the university: the football team, fraternity houses, and so on. Third, remedial language work is given, either on a group or an individual basis as needed in the appropriate area. These are several possible areas on which to focus, depending on the TAs' difficulties.

Pronunciation is a problem with high visibility—TAs often regard it as their highest priority in terms of language remediation. Students frequently cite it as the biggest obstacle to understanding. With TAs from certain countries (India is perhaps the best example), pronunciation problems mar what is otherwise highly proficient speech.

Stress and intonation can cause problems at the level of the word but more difficult to repair are sentence intonation contours borrowed from the mother tongue and used for the same purposes as in the mother tongue. (See the chapter by Zukowski/Faust, this volume, for further discussion of this point.) The work of Montgomery (1976) at the University of Birmingham has shown how important intonation is in dividing up the different subsections of a lecture. In general, intonation is important in English for indicating the relationship of one item of discourse to another.

Vocabulary and word choice are involved because breakdown in communication is often not a sudden and abrupt phenomenon where a teacher produces a sentence and the students say: "We don't understand." It is often a gradual process, where slips in pronunciation combined with inappropriate lexical choice over a stretch of discourse lead to the students finally giving up, but being unable to pinpoint the precise problem. (It is like a slipping vertical hold on the television; if it slips once every five minutes, we can tolerate it; every two minutes becomes uncomfortable and every 20 or 30 seconds is intolerable and we get out of our chair to adjust the set.) For example, a TA trainee began a lecture on the AC motor by remarking that "It is very stout," meaning *sturdy* or *reliable*. No one thought this worth challenging at the time, but it turned out to be the first of a series of small misunderstandings, whose cumulative effect was to destroy the whole presentation.

Sentence structure is important because, while the course can focus on sentence-level representations of functions, such as defining or exemplifying, it obviously cannot teach the entire grammar of English. However, the appearance of fractured relative clauses or misused pronouns may be repaired by individual or group remediation.

Discourse structure is also involved. In a situation where TAs are asked to prepare a detailed lesson plan, it is often easy to point out when and how the language fails to properly represent what has been planned.

Paralinguistic features such as eye contact, gestures, and so on are brought up much more by students in the training program than are syntactic or discoursal errors (which have to be caught in videotape reviews with instructors).

Students often have strong feelings about teachers who avoid eye contact or make inappropriate gestures.

Fourth, remedial pedogogy involves repairing various aspects of the trainee's teaching style. These can range from the selection of examples (aspects of content), and handling questions and interruptions (aspects of classroom management) to structuring a presentation (aspects of the effective transmission of information). An example of the latter was seen when a TA discussed a machine by spending several minutes silently drawing the whole thing on the blackboard. He then attempted to explain how it worked. The students' preference was clearly for a synthetic approach, with each part of the machine being presented, first in isolation and then in relation to the whole.

Finally, remedial language work and pedagogy come together in an interesting way when language deficiencies which can realistically only be remedied in the long run (if ever) can be compensated for by certain pedagogic strategies. Two examples can be offered, both related to the use of the blackboard, specifically its organization.

The normal blackboard procedure is to start somewhere, usually the top left hand corner, and work across the board. When it is crowded or full, erasing makes further writing possible. The blackboard is of tremendous importance to international TAs. We therefore recommend to them that at the beginning of each class they draw two vertical lines, dividing off about one quarter of the space at the two ends. The left-hand space is used to layout the lesson plan: The TA lists the points to be covered, thus compensating in advance for deficiencies in the discourse structure which render the organization of the lesson less than transparent. The right hand section is used for writing technical terms to be used. As each term is used for the first time, it is written on the board. It then remains there for the rest of the class so that the TA can gesture to it whenever the word is used. This strategy compensates for any deficiency in pronunciation which makes unknown or unfamiliar words hard to interpret. The middle section of the blackboard is used for diagrams and other work which can be erased; the two end sections are never erased during the class.

Repair takes place in two ways. The first is spontaneous and arises during and immediately after a teaching assignment. When the TA is giving even a short ten-minute presentation to a group of American students, the feedback (ranging from puzzled frowns to questions, requests for repetition to cries of frustration) can cause the TA to modify his behavior then and there. In the structured feedback session immediately following the practice teaching session, this spontaneous feedback is more clearly articulated and detailed.

The second source of repair involves the trainer. On the individual level, the instructor reviews the videotapes with trainee privately and pulls together the various aspects of the spontaneous feedback, providing additional comments. In this situation, the trainee is usually more comfortable about responding and considering what kind of repair is needed. On a group level, the trainer reviews the feedback being given to the group as a whole and devises activities which will benefit most, if not all, the TAs.

## The Course Model

The course model (presented in Figure 4) is divided into three phases: activities which take place before, during, and after the course. These distinctions are not absolute in that certain pre-course activities may leak into the beginning of the course (establishing the background of the participants, for example) and certain course activities continue after it has finished and the trainee has entered the real world (aspects of feedback and associated repair, for instance). Finally, the post-course activities run into pre-course activities for the next course and the procedure becomes a cycle.

### Pre-course Activities

The pre-course profile is drawn from what was said above about ESP course design. The original motivation for the establishment of such a course came from an outbreak of letters of complaint in the student newspaper. To this can be added interviews with students and a sampling of comments from student evaluations, where these are available. While useful in throwing light on the situation in general (and certainly sampling the emotions involved), these findings can be disappointing in that students are often not able to specify problems beyond poor pronunciation or a general inability to speak the language: "X just can't speak English," "I can't understand a word Y says," and so on.

A second area of activity involves visiting classes taught by international TAs currently involved in instruction. Such observations not only provide the investigator with ideas about what problems are involved but can also lead to fruitful interviews with both the TA and the students in the class. In particular, much more detailed information can be garnered from the students because they and the investigator have a common point of reference, namely the class they have both just experienced. Interviews with the TA are particularly helpful in establishing the kinds of cultural and educational information they would have liked to have had before beginning their teaching in an American university.

These activities can take place some time before the course is given. A third pre-course step is to examine the participants in terms of their linguistic, educational, and cultural background. To be at all complete, this analysis obviously requires a degree of knowledge that even a team of investigators could not have access to. Linguists know a good deal about those differences between English and other languages which tend to interfere in performance. However, this knowledge is usually phonological (speakers of Farsi confuse /v/ and /w/ in English, for example) or syntactic (speakers of Japanese omit articles, for instance) rather than semantic or discoursal. Further, one would not wish to suggest that

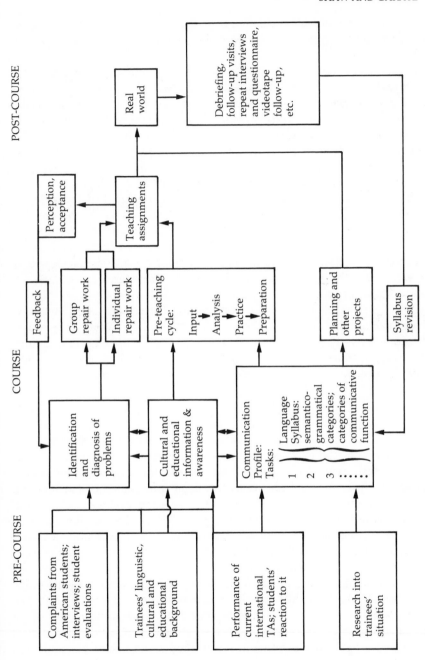

Figure 4. *A model for a training course for international teaching assistants*

a successful international TA training course depends on the course planners and trainers being steeped in knowledge about educational theory and practice in other countries.

In general, the knowledge of the trainee's home educational system together with its culturally determined features will be acquired a posteriori. The more one trains international TAs from various countries, the more one can predict these areas of interference. The experienced trainer will scan the list of countries represented in a particular group of trainees and know what kinds of linguistic, cultural, and educational problems will have to be dealt with. However, we should not depend entirely on this knowledge; it is very easy for stereotypes to be established. Some element of a priori analysis can be achieved by asking trainees to nominate aspects of their home educational and cultural experiences which are most different from the host system. This may be accompanied in the first days of the course by the presentation of relevant aspects of that system. However, this procedure calls for considerable self-knowledge and awareness on the part of the trainee, which may not be available. It may be much later in the course before he is ready to make the necessary comparisons.

The fourth pre-course activity involves finding out exactly what it is that TAs do in different departments. Survey questionnaires, class visits, interviews with department chairpersons and experienced American TAs are all helpful in finding out precisely what is involved. While there is clearly a general element in the training course, the specific skills needed to run a lab course, handle discussion groups, or give supplementary lectures are equally important.

## Course Activities

The course model is based directly on these pre-course activities. Three areas have been defined and fleshed out: the identification and diagnosis of problems, the necessary cultural and educational information and awareness, and the communication profile. The first of these is the least well-defined and will be constantly reassessed during the course, because the problems of individual TAs cannot be accurately predicted from their background; teaching depends so much on individual personality and the way in which that personality interacts with a new environment.

The nature of the second component, on the other hand, remains much more constant. The films, materials, and activities which convey this information and raise awareness do not require drastic modification from one course to the next or one TA to the next. Similarly, the communication profile does not change during the course although, as the model shows, it may be amended on the basis of what is discovered during follow-up activities between courses. The communication profile lists two sets of items: the tasks required of the TA and the language and communication skills needed to fulfill them. Two course components are constructed from these data: the planning and materials prep-aration projects and the pre-teaching cycle.

To take an illustrative example of the latter, the trainees are given a teaching assignment based on one of the language functions identified in the pre-course research: define a significant (but not complex) concept or term from your field. The pre-teaching cycle offers a demonstration of such a piece of teaching, either on videotape or by a trainer. The linguistic and pedagogic realizations are analyzed and rehearsed. Trainees then select their own concept and prepare their mini-lesson. This then leads into the feedback and repair cycle discussed above.

These classroom activities are supported by five projects, which also involve trainees making contact with their department and inspecting materials such as course syllabi, textbooks, and examinations. For the first project, the TA obtains the course outline, syllabus, and textbook provided by the professor and/or department of the course he will teach. The TA completes a calendar for the semester including the first meeting for the course, the assignments, holi-days that could conflict with assignments, and the TA's personal class schedule. The TA writes behavioral objectives for each unit in the course. The second project involves a unit plan. The TA outlines each class period within a given unit. Behavioral objectives are clarified at this point. This is followed by a testing project in which the TA writes test items for a given unit. Lecture and class discussion provide the TA with an overview of testing/evaluation theory, sam-ple tests, and appropriate testing devices. The fourth project involves lesson planning. The TA writes a lesson plan for three consecutive classes. Attention is paid to time constraints, sequencing, teacher/student activities, classroom organization, and variation of teaching style. The final project calls for the planning and production of a visual aid for use in one of the planned lessons or in a teaching assignment.

## Post-course Activities

Finally, the model calls for the trainees to be followed into the real world of university teaching. Debriefing should take place at several points: immedi-ately after the course, after one semester, after one year. At each point, the trainees' perceptions of what they wanted from the course and what was most valuable change perceptibly, although the teaching-feedback cycle is always regarded as the most significant and valuable part of the course. Observation of trainees in action is useful, not only for the trainees, who are given further support and help in their teaching, but also for the trainer, who is constantly reevaluating and redesigning the course.

This model is only one of a number of viable approaches to the training of international teaching assistants in American universities. It has proved a fruit-ful and stimulating basis for training activities. In the long run, one of the most useful features is the capacity to incorporate change both during the course and between one course and the next, as our knowledge of the nature of the problem and of possible solutions increases.

## Endnotes

1. Portions of this chapter were presented at the Annual CATESOL State Conference in San Diego (Cheney-Rice, Garate, and Shaw 1980a), and the Annual NAFSA Conference in St. Louis (Cheney-Rice, Garate, and Shaw 1980b).

2. Of course, unsuccessful communication is seldom entirely one-sided. For a discussion of the students' role in the foreign TA problem, see Bailey's paper, "A Typology of Teaching Assistants" (this volume).

# Part II
## *The Programs*

# A Survey of Training Programs for Foreign Teaching Assistants in American Universities[1]

## Nina J. Turitz

*I*n the fall of 1982, fifteen universities were surveyed which now have, or have had, programs designed to upgrade the language, cultural sophisti- cation, and teaching skills of foreign TAs. The purpose of the survey was to find out how the programs were set up, what their objectives were, and how they had been received, in order that institutions considering the establishment of such programs might benefit from this knowledge. In this chapter, the findings of the survey are summarized.

## Institutional Responses

The fifteen institutions listed in Appendix A were identified from a mailing list of people interested in non-native speaking teaching assistants.[2] In all, questionnaires were sent to approximately forty institutions. Twenty-five insti- tutions (63 percent) returned the questionnaire; of these seven had no program and anticipated none in the future, and four had no program but anticipated the need for one. The names and addresses of the contact persons who responded to the questionnaire are given in Appendix A.

The foreign TA training programs at the remaining fifteen institutions can be divided into two basic types: the seminar-type and the orientation type. The seminar-type program meets throughout the term for a given number of hours per week; the orientation-type meets for a short period of time prior to the beginning of the foreign TA's first term.

Twelve responding institutions offer seminar-type training programs. Two of these, however, have been discontinued: that of the University of California at Berkeley, because of insufficient enrollment and lack of support from the departments involved, and that of the University of Houston, because of lack of funding. All of the programs run for one term—a semester or a quarter—with the exception of the Oregon State program, which runs for one year.

Only three institutions responding to the survey offer orientation-type programs. These vary in length from one and a half weeks to three weeks and offer from nine to ninety instructional hours. (See Table 1.) All of the training programs of both types are relatively new. The oldest is that at the University of California at Berkeley (since discontinued), established in 1976, while the newest among the responding schools are those at Stanford University and Northeastern University, both established in 1982.

Table 1. *Orientation programs: Length and total instructional hours*

| Program | Length of program | Total hours of instruction |
|---------|-------------------|----------------------------|
| Cornell | Two weeks | 30+ |
| Northeastern | Eight days | (not reported) |
| Texas Tech | Three weeks | 90 |

## Direction, Staffing, and Funding

There is considerable variation in the direction and staffing of the foreign TA training programs. Seven are directed and staffed by the university's English as a Foreign Language (EFL) program alone; five by the EFL program in conjunction with another part of the university; and two by offices of instructional development. (See Table 2.)

Table 2. *Direction and staffing*

| Program | Source of staffing |
|---------|--------------------|
| Arizona State | English Skills Program and Communications Department under the auspices of the Program for Faculty Development |
| UC Berkeley | ESL Department |
| UC Davis | Teaching Resources Center |
| UC Los Angeles | ESL Department |
| Houston | ESL Department |
| Illinois at Champaign/Urbana | Division of ESL |
| Indiana | English Language Improvement Program, Department of Linguistics |
| Minnesota | ESL Program (Linguistics Department) |
| Ohio | Ohio Program of Intensive English |
| Oregon State | Instructional Development Center |
| Pennsylvania State | Center for ESL |
| Stanford | English for Foreign Students and Center for Teaching and Learning |
| Cornell* | Intensive English Program |
| Northeastern* | English Language Center and Office of Learning Resources |
| Texas Tech* | ESOL Program, Speech and Communication Department, and International Programs |

*Orientation-type programs

In most of the institutions responding to the survey, the program is provided at no cost to the foreign graduate students enrolled, although in some
programs the foreign TAs are required to cover their living expenses prior to
the term (Northeastern University) or to buy materials (Ohio University). Funding is provided in a variety of ways. In two cases, the EFL program alone covers
the costs of the program. In three others, the Office of Instructional Development provides the funds. Other offices of the university provide the funding
for five programs, and in two cases funding is provided by a grant. (See Table
3.).

Table 3. *Types of funding*

| Program | Source of funding |
| --- | --- |
| Arizona State | University Program for Faculty Development |
| UC Berkeley | Special grant (source not indicated) |
| UC Davis | Teaching Resources Center |
| UC Los Angeles | Office of Instructional Development (special instructional improve-ment funds) |
| Houston | (Source not indicated) |
| Illinois at Champaign/Urbana | ESL Division with some support from the School of Humanities, Liberal Arts and Sciences |
| Indiana | English Language Improvement Program |
| Minnesota | Students' departments, 50%; Academic Affairs, 50% |
| Ohio | Ohio Program of Intensive English |
| Oregon State | Undergraduate and Graduate Studies |
| Pennsylvania State | Provost, Liberal Arts, Graduate School |
| Stanford | Humanities and Sciences, Graduate Studies |
| Cornell* | Exxon Foundation |
| Northeastern* | Provost's Office |
| Texas Tech* | Vice President for Academic Affairs |

*Orientation-type programs

## Hours of Instruction, Credit, and Participation

In the seminar programs, the number of hours of instruction per week
varies from one to six. Approximately half of the seminar-type programs offer
credit for participation. None of the orientation-type programs do, however.
(See Table 4.)

Participation in the training programs is optional at the majority of institutions responding to the survey, although it is mandatory in three cases.
Participation may be limited to current TAs or to prospective TAs, or may
include both, as shown in Table 5.

### Objectives and Materials

Program objectives may include linguistic, cultural, and pedagogical goals,
as depicted in Table 6. The majority of the programs responding to the survey

Table 4. *Credit and Hours of Instruction in Seminar-Type Programs*

| Program | Credit | Hours of instruction |
|---|---|---|
| Arizona State | None | 2 classroom hours plus 1 hour of individual instruction as needed |
| UC Berkeley | 2 units discontinued | 3 |
| UC Davis | 2 units | 2 |
| UC Los Angeles | 4 quarter units | 4 |
| Houston | (Discontinued) | 3 classroom hours plus individual consultations |
| Illinois at Champaign/Urbana | None | 2 |
| Indiana | None | 3 |
| Minnesota | None | 3 |
| Ohio | 2 units | 4 |
| Oregon State | None | 1-3 |
| Pennsylvania State | 3 units | 4.5 |
| Stanford | 2 units | 2 classroom hours and individual consultations as needed |

Table 5. *Program participation*

| Program | Participants | Optional/Mandatory |
|---|---|---|
| Arizona State | Current TAs selected by their department chairmen or academic advisers | O |
| UC Berkeley | Current TAs | O |
| UC Davis | Prospective TAs | O |
| UC Los Angeles | 1. Current TAs<br>2. Other graduate students<br>3. All others | O |
| Houston | Current TAs | M |
| Illinois at Champaign/Urbana | Current and prospective TAs | O (M for physics TAs) |
| Indiana | Prospective TAs with at least 550 TOEFL score | O |
| Minnesota | Current and prospective TAs | O (some departments may require it) |
| Ohio | Current TAs who have completed other language training (with at least 78 MTELP) | O |
| Oregon State | Current TAs nominated by their departments | O |
| Pennsylvania State | Current TAs with less than 250 TSE | M |
| Stanford | Current and prospective TAs | O |
| Cornell* | Current TAs (enrollment limited to 12) | O |
| Northeastern* | All new international TAs who have not been TAs in another program | M |
| Texas Tech* | Current TAs; prospective TAs if space is available | M |

*Orientation-type programs

Table 6. *Program objectives*

| Program | Language | Culture | Pedagogy |
|---|---|---|---|
| Arizona State | Yes | Yes | Yes |
| UC Berkeley | Not specifically | Some | Yes |
| UC Davis | Minimal | Yes | Yes |
| UC Los Angeles | Yes | Some | Some |
| Houston | Yes | Yes | Yes |
| Illinois at Champaign/Urbana | Yes | No | Yes |
| Indiana | Yes | (Needs met by departments) | |
| Minnesota | Yes | Yes | Yes |
| Ohio | Yes | Yes | Yes |
| Oregon State | No | Yes | Yes |
| Pennsylvania State | Yes | Yes | Minimal |
| Stanford | Yes | Yes | Yes |
| Cornell* | Yes | Yes | Yes |
| Northeastern* | Yes | Yes | Yes |
| Texas Tech* | Yes | Yes | Yes |

*Orientation-type programs

cover all three elements, including the orientation programs, which appear to be not long enough to make a real difference in the participants' English proficiency. (See the chapter by Gaskill and Brinton in this volume for further discussion of this point.)

In most of the programs, practice lessons taught by the participants are videotaped for review by the TAs. The University of Houston program requires its TAs to tape, transcribe, and analyze an actual class session; Northeastern University shows its participants videotapes of American teachers in class. About half of the programs use a text or manual. The others either use teacher-made materials or did not specify in the survey what materials were used. (See Table 7.)

## Responses to the Training Programs

Most responding institutions report a favorable reception to the training programs by the foreign TAs who participate. (See Table 8.) Departmental reaction is generally good also, but there is little information on whether the undergraduates, whose complaints provided the motivation to institute the programs, are satisfied. Only the questionnaire from Oregon State University reported a response ("excellent") on the part of undergraduate students.

Since undergraduate input could be invaluable in developing and improving the training programs, and positive evaluations from undergraduate students could be indicative of a program's success, it is important for those of us who are involved in these programs to solicit students' input.[3] One program which does this is that at Oregon State University. According to Dean Osterman,

Table 7. *Materials and activities used in TA training programs*

| Program | Materials and activities |
| --- | --- |
| Arizona State | Levine and Adelman, *Beyond Language*; teacher-made materials |
| UC Berkeley | No materials specified |
| UC Davis | Parts of various texts on public speaking |
| UC Los Angeles | Videotaping; role plays; Rodman, *Public Speaking* |
| Houston | Videotaping; role plays; essays; discussions |
| Illinois at Champaign/Urbana | Videotaping; discussions; role plays; Rodman, *Public Speaking* |
| Indiana | No materials specified |
| Minnesota | Videotaping; various ESL materials in individual tutorials |
| Ohio | Videotaping; Morley, *Improving Spoken English*, Vol. 1; TAs' class texts |
| Oregon State | Microteaching, cognitive maps, feedback, lectures |
| Pennsylvania State | Videotaping |
| Stanford | Videotaping; Keller and Warner, *Gambits 2:Links*; Fisher, *Teaching at Stanford* |
| Cornell* | Videotaping |
| Northeastern* | Videotaping; Althen, *Manual for Foreign TAs*; Keller and Warner, *Gambits* |
| Texas Tech* | Materials vary |

*Orientation-type programs

Table 8. *Response to the training program*

| Program | Participants | Departments |
| --- | --- | --- |
| Arizona State | Very good | Good |
| UC Berkeley | Good | Mixed |
| UC Davis | Great | Mixed |
| UC Los Angeles | (Not specified) | (Not specified) |
| Houston | (Not specified) | (Not specified) |
| Illinois at Champaign/Urbana | Favorable | Favorable |
| Indiana | Mixed | Good |
| Minnesota | Excellent | Favorable |
| Ohio | Excellent | Excellent |
| Oregon State | Excellent | Excellent |
| Pennsylvania State | Favorable | Neutral |
| Stanford | Enthusiastic | Enthusiastic |
| Cornell* | Extremely good | So-so |
| Northeastern* | Very favorable | (Not specified) |
| Texas Tech* | Generally good | Enthusiastic |

*Orientation-type programs

Director of Instructional and Faculty Development, undergraduates at OSU have the opportunity to influence how their classes are taught via "small group instructional diagnosis." Midway through the term, Osterman visits selected classes and solicits reactions as to what the students like about the class as it has been taught so far and what they would like changed. The class as a whole must agree (by vote) on the final list of changes. Then Osterman meets privately with the TA to discuss his findings and to suggest what the TA might do to improve.

Osterman reports that TAs (both foreign and American) tend to be rated higher in these sessions if they have been through the Instructional Development Center's training program. OSU undergraduates also fill out a standard written evaluation of their TAs at the end of the term. According to Osterman, there are again "significant differences," with TAs who participated in the training program being rated more favorably than those who did not.

The value in small group instructional diagnosis lies in its positive approach. It elicits concrete suggestions for positive action during the semester, when changes can still be effected. The Oregon State model might be a good one for other universities to follow.

## Conclusions

The findings of this admittedly limited survey seem to indicate that existing foreign TA training programs are generally well received by both participants and departments. However, cooperation and proper funding are essential if such training programs are to succeed.

First, the various departments, institutes, and offices of the university need to work together to set up the program and ensure that those who need it enroll. These offices include the graduate departments employing foreign TAs, the administration, the EFL program, and other members of the university community, such as the instructional development office.

Second, it must be recognized that it is in the interest of the university as a whole to support programs whose goal it is to raise the standards of undergraduate instruction. If the EFL program is expected to absorb the entire cost of the training program, as in the case of the University of Houston, the program may be doomed to failure.

It is still too early to evaluate the actual effectiveness of foreign TA training and orientation programs, but objective evaluations of such programs are needed. They will enable us to improve the programs and their usefulness to the departments and the adminstration, and they will provide institutions considering such programs with evidence of their value. Possible bases for such evaluations might include student evaluations of foreign TAs, statistics on courses and sections dropped by undergraduates, measures of student achievement,[4] participant and department evaluations, and follow-up evaluations later in the foreign TAs' tenure. (The paper by Landa and Perry in this volume provides an example of one such long-term follow-up evaluation.)

## Endnotes

1. This chapter is based on the author's presentation at the Regional NAFSA Region VIII Conference held in Easton, Maryland, in December 1982.

2. This computerized mailing list is maintained by Kathleen M. Bailey, co-editor of this volume. Inquiries should be sent to her at the Monterey Institute of International Studies.

3. In research conducted at UCLA (Hinofotis and Bailey 1981), freshmen rated randomly ordered videotapes of potential foreign teaching assistants filmed before and after they had completed a forty-hour seminar-type course in oral communication. The undergraduate raters, like a sample of ESL teachers and TA trainers in an earlier study (Hinofotis, Bailey and Stern, 1979), perceived statistically significant improvement in the foreign TAs' oral communication skills in the post-treatment videotapes. These findings suggest that perceptible improvement is possible in a relatively short period of time, but the authors note that since no control group was available, the improvement cannot be attributed unambiguously to the foreign TA training program.

In a study conducted at the University of Minnesota, Keye also measured changes in the evaluations of foreign teaching assistants by American students, following a forty-hour, ten-week training course. She concluded that "training did affect improvement in . . . language skills, teaching effectiveness, and cross-cultural awareness in the U.S. classroom setting" (1981, 2).

4. See Jacobs and Friedman (forthcoming) for a comparison of student achievement in classes taught by foreign TAs and native English speaking TAs at Indiana University.

## Appendix A.  *Contact people at the responding institutions*

*Seminar-type programs*

William Acton, Assistant Professor, Dept. of English, University of Houston, Houston, TX 77004; (713) 749-3431.

Richard R. Bier, Coordinator, English Language Improvement Program, Dept. of Linguistics, Indiana University, Bloomington, IN 47405; (812) 335-0033.

H. Douglas Brown, Director, Division of English as a Second Language, University of Illinois, 707 South Mathews, Urbana, IL 61801.

Sandra Colombo, Acting Director, University Program for Faculty Development, A-139 Ritter, Arizona State University, Tempe, AZ 85287; (602) 965-6739.

Marion R. Franck, Lecturer, Rhetoric Dept., University of California, Davis, CA 95616.

John Hinds, Director, Center for ESL, 305 Sparks Building, Pennsylvania State University, University Park, PA 16802; (814) 865-7365.

Mark Landa, Director, English Program for International Students, 152 Klaeber Court, 3230 16th Avenue SE, Minneapolis, Minnesota 55455.

Larry L. Loeher, Director, Office of Instructional Development, 70 Powell Library, University of California, Los Angeles, CA 90024; (213) 825-5244.

Beverley McChesney, Director, English for Foreign Students, Building 100, Stanford University, Stanford, CA 94305; (415) 497-3636.

June McKay, ESL Coordinator, T-2241, University of California, Berkeley, CA 94720; (415) 642-5975.

Dean N. Osterman, Director, Instructional and Faculty Development, Instructional Development Center, Oregon State University, Corvallis, Oregon 97331; (503) 754-4335.

Adelaide Heyde Parsons, Director, Ohio Program of Intensive English, 201 Gordy Hall, Ohio University, Athens, OH 45701; (614) 594-5634.

*Orientation-type programs*

Erik J. Beukenkamp, Director, Intensive English Program, Morrill Hall, Cornell University, Ithaca, NY 14853.

Paul C. Krueger, Assistant Dean/Director, English Language Center, 206 Boston YMCA, 360 Huntington Avenue, Boston, MA 02115; (607) 437-2455.

Rosslyn Smith, Director, ESOL Program, Dept. of Classical and Romance Languages, Texas Tech University, Lubbock, TX 79409-4649.

# A One-day Workshop in Oral Communication Skills[1]

## KATHLEEN M. BAILEY
## FRANCES B. HINOFOTIS

*T*his chapter describes a one-day workshop in oral communication skills
that was offered for international visiting scholars at the University of
California at Los Angeles (UCLA). However, the activities outlined here
could be used in a brief orientation-type training program (Turitz, this volume)
for foreign teaching assistants where departments do not have financial support
for longer seminar-type programs.

The workshop was offered on a trial basis by UCLA's Office of Instructional
Development in conjunction with the ESL Section. It was based on activities
used in a ten-week course in advanced oral communication (Hinofotis and
Bailey 1978) that had been developed in part to help foreign TAs improve their
English language communication skills. The workshop activities and the participants' and leaders' reactions to them are discussed in some detail here so
that they may serve as a model for people interested in offering similar programs.

## Participants

Workshop members volunteered to participate after learning about the
one-day program through their departments. The Office of Instructional Development sent invitations to department chairpersons, who informed the visiting
scholars in their departments. In other words, attendance at this particular
workshop was not required though some participants may have been strongly
encouraged to attend by their host departments.

The workshop was attended by twelve scholars from seven different
countries: France, Japan, South Korea, the Netherlands, West Germany, the
U.S.S.R., and the People's Republic of China. Academic disciplines of the group

51

members included Dutch literature, computer science, anesthesiology, radiology, English literature, geophysics, engineering, and immigration law. Thus the participants represented a variety of interests and native language backgrounds.

## Workshop Goals and Activities

The oral communication workshop had three main purposes:
1. to acquaint the visiting scholars with the characteristics of effective oral communication in English;
2. to give the scholars guided practice in making oral presentations before an audience and in responding to questions following the presentations;
3. to provide the scholars with both videotape feedback and the workshop leaders' suggestions for improving their oral communication skills.

As these goals suggest, the workshop was intended primarily as a consciousness-raising and information session, rather than as the only guidance the participants would receive. (Obviously relatively little can be accomplished in one day.) The activities described briefly below were planned in order to achieve these goals.

The workshop was held in a comfortable room at the UCLA Faculty Center. Such a facility is ideal for this type of program because it typically has informal furniture for the small-group and dyad activities, as well as tables, chairs, a blackboard, and a podium for more formal presentations, and because of the the available food services. On the day of the workshop, coffee breaks and a luncheon allowed time for the visiting scholars to interact informally. Because many of them found casual conversation somewhat difficult, these relaxed periods proved useful.

At the beginning of the day's activities, each participant completed an information sheet. (A copy of this form is given in Appendix A.) Among other things, the scholars were asked to identify their own strengths and weaknesses in English. Those areas most often cited as strong points included reading, grammar, and technical or subject-specific vocabulary. Areas identified as needing improvement were pronunciation, conversational skills, and the ability to understand spoken English.

Four of the participants (one third) expressed a desire to increase their vocabularies in the area of colloquial English. For this reason, an emphasis on vocabulary and idioms was added to the day's activities. Each time an idiom or an apparently new vocabulary item was used and discussed, one of the workshop leaders noted the term or phrase. The collection of terms was later typed with definitions and examples. This list was distributed to the participants when they came to view their videotapes privately the next week.

After the information sheets had been completed the two facilitators introduced each other and briefly outlined the day's program. These introductory remarks served the dual function of putting the participants at ease and providing them with models for the next activity: introducing one another.

For the peer introductions, each participant was paired with a partner from a different discipline and language background. The scholars spent five to ten minutes interviewing their partners, making brief notes as needed on index cards. Then each scholar stood before the group and introduced his partner. This activity provided the participants with information about one another and with an initial "public speaking" experience in which the focus of their talk was not on their own ideas or experiences.

The introductions were followed by model presentations by the two workshop leaders. The same speech, which dealt with cultural differences, was given twice—first poorly and then well. (For a discussion of this activity in a foreign TA training program, see Gaskill and Brinton, this volume.) The group discussed the good and bad presentations with one facilitator listing "do's" and "don't's" on the blackboard as the participants identified the problems and strengths of the two deliveries. Thus the scholars themselves, based on their own experience as audience members, generated a list of behaviors to practice or avoid when speaking to an audience.

The next scheduled activity consisted of impromptu speeches. The plan was for each scholar to draw a topic (from a list prepared in advance) dealing with culture in academe. (See Appendix B for a list of such topics.) After one minute of preparation, each participant would speak for three minutes on the topic he had selected. Then the workshop leaders and other participants would ask questions and comment immediately after each impromptu speech. However, because twelve visiting scholars attended the program, which had been planned for ten participants, all the activities took longer than anticipated and the three-minute impromptu speeches had to be cut from the program. In light of this problem, such a workshop should probably be limited to ten participants or fewer.

Following a one-hour lunch break, the afternoon session was devoted to extemporaneous speeches. Each scholar took about ten minutes to prepare a five-minute talk explaining a concept or technical term from his area of specialization. The two workshop leaders circulated and supplied vocabulary or grammar help as needed. The scholars' presentations were professionally videotaped so that they could see themselves later. This arrangement also freed the two workshop leaders from videotaping responsibilities to concentrate on evaluating the presentations.

As each scholar spoke, the two workshop leaders independently noted pronunciation problems, grammatical and lexical errors, distracting nonverbal behaviors, and apparent strengths in the scholars' oral English. These items were noted on a checklist adapted from one used in the ten-week oral communication course. (See Appendix C for a copy of the checklist.) Both leaders' written comments were given to the individual scholars when they viewed the videotape with one of the workshop leaders during the following week. After each extemporaneous speech, the workshop leaders and the other participants asked questions about the topic.

## Evaluation of the Workshop

At the end of the day-long program, the visiting scholars were asked to complete a brief evaluation form. The items and the results are summarized in Table 1. Those items dealing with the impromptu speeches have been deleted from the evaluation since that activity had to be cancelled because of lack of time. Each scholar had the opportunity to add to or change his ratings on the evaluation form after viewing the videotape of his extemporaneous speech.

Table 1. *Visiting scholars' evaluation of the workshop in oral communication*

| Likert scale item | Mean | Standard Deviation |
|---|---|---|
| 1. The workshop was helpful to me. | 4.42 | .51 |
| 2. The introductions helped me get to know my colleagues. | 4.36 | .81 |
| 3. The demonstration speeches of good and poor speaking manners were useful. | 4.27 | .90 |
| 4. The discussion of cultural aspects of oral communication was useful and informative | 3.92 | .79 |
| 5. Giving my extemporaneous speech was good practice for me. | 4.25 | .62 |
| 6. The checklist we used helped me identify my strengths and weaknesses in oral communication in English. | 4.17 | .98 |
| 7. Listening to my colleagues' speeches was useful in helping me see my own problems and strengths in oral communication. | 3.83 | .72 |
| 8. Answering questions from an audience is difficult for me. | 2.73 | 1.19 |
| 9. Answering questions from the group after giving my extemporaneous speech was good practice for me. | 4.00 | .95 |
| 10. Being videotaped made me nervous. | 2.17 | .72 |
| 11. Being videotaped was a good experience. | 3.83 | .94 |
| 12. It will probably be useful to see myself on videotape. | 4.40 | .52 |
| 13. I would recommend this oral communication workshop to other visiting scholars at UCLA. | 4.64 | .50 |
| 14. The workshop leaders were helpful and well-organized. | 4.42 | .51 |

Scores were computed on a five-point scale: 1 = strongly disagree, 2 = disagree, 4 = agree, 5 = strongly agree (n = 12).

Some conclusions can be drawn from these data. The respondents were largely a confident group, although their English proficiency varied considerably. In general, the videotaping did not seem to bother them, nor did they seem to experience much anxiety in answering questions. However, responding to questions from the audience generated the widest range of responses (as shown by the standard deviation for Item 8 in Table 1), indicating a variety of reactions among the visiting scholars on this point. The overall ratings of the program were high, with the leaders and the workshop in general both receiving a mean score of 4.42 on a five-point scale. The participants all agreed or strongly agreed (4.64) with the statement, "I would recommend the oral communication workshop to other visiting scholars at UCLA."

The specific activities that were judged useful were seeing oneself on videotape (4.40), introductions of colleagues (4.36), watching the demonstration speeches (4.27), use of the checklist (4.17), and answering questions from the audience (4.00). Activities that were judged to be less useful included the discussion of cultural aspects of oral communication (3.92) and listening to one another's extemporaneous speeches (3.83). There was also a variety of responses to the statement, "Being videotaped was a good experience" (3.83).

The evaluation form also included four open-ended questions and a space for optional comments:

1. What workshop activity helped you the most? Why?
2. What activity was least helpful? Why?
3. What are your overall impressions of the oral communication workshop?
4. What suggestions would you make for improving the workshop?

Most participants responded to the first two questions with positive comments; negative comments centered on listening to other non-native speakers. General overall impressions were unanimously positive. Suggestions for improvement included expansion of the program, ideas about specific techniques, and more interaction between course instructors and individual participants.

Based on these comments and the ratings given in Table 1, the leaders agree that the demonstration speeches could be shortened without loss of effectiveness, that the workshop could be offered for scholars or teaching assistants from specific fields, and that faculty members or students should be invited to participate in the program as peer coaches or members of the audience. Furthermore, any workshop of this sort should probably be limited to eight or ten participants, which would allow each one more "talk-time" while also permitting a wider variety of activities. In addition, the extemporaneous speeches should be limited or presented as two groups to half-group audiences to prevent restlessness and to maintain a high level of critical awareness.

Any discussion of the efficacy of such a program must also include budget questions. The cost can be broken down into two main areas: media support and facilities costs. Media support includes the camera professional, videotapes, and the rental of videotaping equipment. Facilities costs include room rental and food services. People planning similar workshops should also consider workshop leaders' fees, where these sorts of activities are not part of their regular instructional responsibilities.

It would be impossible to judge the effectiveness of such a program accurately without obtaining pre- and post-treatment videotapes and using a control group that did not participate in the workshop. However, it is clear from the participants' reactions that the oral communication workshop had a high level of face validity: the visiting scholars believed they were being helped. Because none of the twelve participants had been videotaped before, that in itself was a learning experience. They also seemed to benefit from the individual consultation time spent in reviewing their videotapes with them and in going over the diagnostic points on the checklists filled out by the workshop leaders.

## Concluding Remarks

International visiting scholars represent a vast and probably under-used educational asset in U.S. universities. If a workshop such as the one described here can help them gain the confidence to speak up and communicate more with students and faculty members in their departments, the increased communication could lead to a richer educational experience for the students and faculty of the host institution as well as for the scholars themselves.

This sort of oral communication workshop could also prove useful in orientation-type training sessions for foreign TAs, particularly in situations where lack of time and financial resources will not permit longer programs. The workshop could be offered on a departmental basis and be staffed by faculty members charged with TA supervision, provided they themselves were fluent speakers of English and effective teachers. Or workshop leaders from ESL or speech/communications departments could assist departmental faculty members in providing specific feedback to the TAs, either at the workshop itself or during the later videotape viewing sessions.

It is important to note, however, that unlike visiting scholars, who may avoid interaction with American undergraduates if they choose, foreign TAs must be able to communicate with both students and faculty members. A day-long program, no matter how effective it may be, is only a first step. Except in the cases of foreign TA trainees with a fair degree of English proficiency and considerable familiarity with the teaching behaviors preferred in U.S. classrooms, a one-day workshop cannot be expected to do more than raise the TAs' awareness of their own behavior and how it may differ from (or coincide with) the oral communication skills of an effective teacher in this culture.

There is at least one preventive benefit of offering an oral communication workshop as part of an orientation-type program for new foreign teaching assistants. That is, in the absence of other screening devices or standards, seeing the performance of non-native speaking TAs in the various activities described above would give the workshop leaders a first-hand impression of which TAs could probably handle teaching assignments immediately and which should be advised to seek further help (e.g., in longer seminar-type programs) while being given tutoring or paper-grading tasks rather than classroom teaching responsibilities.

# Endnotes

1. An earlier version of this paper was presented at the Annual NAFSA Conference in St. Louis, Missouri, May 20-23, 1980.

## Appendix A. *Participant information sheet*

1. What is your full name? (Family name, given name)
2. What name do you prefer to be called during the workshop?
3. What is your native language?
4. What other language(s) do you speak?
5. What department are you visiting at UCLA this year?
6. What is your own area of professional specialization?
7. Will you be teaching a course (or courses) at UCLA this year? If so, what course(s)?
8. Will you be giving guest lectures to UCLA or other groups this year? If so, please describe the topics or the groups you anticipate speaking for.
9. How did you learn about today's oral communication workshop?
10. Are you a teacher or a university professor in your home country? If so, where do you teach and what subjects do you teach?
11. What are your strong points in English?
12. In what areas do you think your English could be improved?
13. What do you hope to gain from your participation in this workshop? (If you need additional space, please use the back of this page to answer the question.)

## Appendix B. *Sample topics for impromptu speeches*

1. Describe the grading system in your country and compare it to what you know about the grading system in the United States.
2. Describe the relationship between professors and college students in your home country.
3. How important is it to have a college degree in your country? Why?
4. What are the major concerns (social, personal, academic, political) of students in your home country?
5. What are your early impressions of the students in the department you are visiting this year?
6. What is your idea of an educated person? Have you ever met anyone who didn't go to high school but whom you considered to be educated? (Explain.)
7. How is your academic life here different from the way it was in your home country?
8. Should it be the professor's responsibility to motivate students at the university level? Why or why not?
9. Should effort and attendance be taken into consideration in the students' final grades in university classes? How would you grade a student who put forth a great deal of effort and attended every class but failed the final examination?
10. What professional or academic experience do you hope to gain in your host department this year?
11. How can the research facilities in your host department and at this university in general be of help to you in your own area of specialization?
12. How is the physical layout of your host department (for example, the office space, the classrooms, the surrounding areas) similar to or different from your department at your home university?

13. What courses do you plan to attend during your stay here and why have you chosen these courses? How will they be of use to you in your long-range academic career?

## Appendix C. *Evaluation of visiting scholars' speeches**

I. Delivery
   A. Visual aspects (eye contact, movement, posture, gestures, facial expressions, etc.)
   B. Auditory aspects (volume, pitch, rate, articulation, clarity, etc.)
   C. Pronunciation
   D. Grammar
II. Content
   A. Organization of speech (introduction, body, transitional expressions, conclusion)
   B. Information (content explained, information conveyed to audience)
   C. Interest level (audience interest maintained, use of humor or examples, illustrations given, etc.)
III. Overall comments
   A. Suggestions for improvement
   B. Strengths of the presentation

*This evaluation checklist was adapted from one used in an advanced oral communication course taught by Susan Stern at UCLA.

# A One-week Language Skills Orientation Program for Foreign Teaching Assistants and Graduate Students[1]

WILLIAM GASKILL
DONNA BRINTON

*P* resented with a growing population of foreign teaching assistants (TAs) as well as complaints from undergraduates about foreign TA intelligibility, administrators at the University of California at Irvine (UCI) decided to institute a program aimed at increasing the classroom effectiveness of foreign TAs. The program was envisioned as having two separate phases: an intensive one-week program to be held during fall orientation week and an ongoing program to be offered throughout the academic year.

Early in the planning stage, an administrative decision was made to expand the one-week orientation to include both TA and non-TA foreign graduate students. Thus the original conception of the program was modified. This chapter details the following aspects of the one-week orientation program:

1. the student population involved;
2. the rationale for the syllabus;
3. the use of videotape recordings to improve student presentation techniques;
4. video playback of university lectures;
5. simulated testing situations;
6. communication exercises of a role-playing and problem-solving nature;
7. student evaluations;
8. suggestions for similar programs.

## Student Population

The student population of the program was highly heterogeneous. In addition to the approximately equal numbers of TA and non-TA participants, the students in the program came from a wide variety of linguistic, cultural, and academic backgrounds. Of the twenty-nine students involved in the orientation program, seventeen had studied previously at American universities, and a number of these were returning rather than incoming students at UCI. Another difference involved the proficiency of the participants. As determined by the UCLA English as a Second Language Proficiency Examination (ESLPE), their English proficiency ranged from beginning (n = 3) and intermediate (n = 6) to advanced (n = 10). Seven of the students scored high enough to have been exempted from required ESL courses at UCLA.

## Needs Analysis

Because of time constraints and the unavailability of participants, it was not feasible to conduct a formal needs analysis of the student population prior to the syllabus design phase. However, where possible we collected background data, such as names of students, native countries, language backgrounds, and major fields of study. Since, at the time, there was no existing ESL program at UCI, the ESL activities were coordinated through the Learning Skills Center. We were able to obtain relevant information on the general foreign student population from the instructors and counselors at the center. This information, added to our own experiences with similar foreign student populations on the UCLA campus, proved valuable in developing the program syllabus.

## Program Logistics

Many problems which arose in the program planning stage involved issues such as how to divide the students into two groups of approximately equal size, which instructor to assign to which group, and how to arrange class sessions so that they would not conflict with other orientation week activities. Though routine for the most part, the problems of program planning were compounded by the heterogeneous character of the student population.

While initial consideration was given to dividing the groups according to TA/non-TA status, or to dividing them into two levels of proficiency, we decided instead to divide the two groups randomly, and to change the group rosters on a day-to-day basis. This decision was based on our belief that by mixing more proficient students with less proficient ones, there would be a greater opportunity for peer instruction. Additionally, we felt that by daily reassigning students to groups, social interaction among students would be increased. Finally, it was our hope that dividing the two groups in this way would avoid the stigma associated with being placed in the "lower" of two groups.

The problem of how to assign instructors to groups solved itself in that some activities seemed conducive to team teaching with one large group while other activities, such as videotaping, required smaller groups. Thus for these activities, we divided students into two classes with each instructor supervising the same activity twice; students then rotated from instructor to instructor (see Figure 1).

## Curriculum Decisions

The administrative decision to open the orientation program to non-TAs complicated curriculum planning. Although the original aim of the program—to increase TA effectiveness—was called into question by this change, we felt that the immediacy of TA needs justified retaining some of the original emphasis. Nonetheless, in light of the addition of non-TAs to the population, and given the dual student/teacher role of TAs, we decided to expand the focus of the program to address both the academic needs of graduate students and the teaching-oriented needs of TAs.

Realizing that within one week all we could hope to do was to touch on skill areas required by both groups, we decided to emphasize oral and listening skills needed in an academic environment. Thus only one session related to grammar. This session was entitled "focus on question formation" and included a review of question word order in direct and embedded questions. We felt that both TAs and graduate students needed to be proficient in question formation, and our past experience had taught us that students at all levels of proficiency have difficulty with this area of English grammar.

To meet the needs of TAs, we drew heavily on the precedents set by UCLA's advanced oral communication course (see Hinofotis and Bailey 1978). That course utilized videotape recordings extensively. We felt that this medium could play a powerful role in helping TAs identify problems in their own presentation techniques and communication strategies. In meeting the student-oriented needs of both TAs and non-TAs, we decided to further capitalize on the medium of videotape by showing previously recorded lectures, thereby providing students with listening and note-taking experience. In sum, practice in the following areas seemed most appropriate in meeting the needs of the orientation program participants:

1. organizing and presenting brief talks related to the student's major field;
2. asking and answering questions based on such presentations;
3. comprehending university lectures;
4. taking notes on university lecture material;
5. preparing for multiple choice and essay type exams based on such material;
6. communicating with student peers and professors in an academic framework;
7. adjusting culturally to the immediate academic and non-academic environment.[2]

## Administration of the ESLPE

Despite our decision to integrate the different proficiency levels, we felt that it would be valuable to administer the ESLPE on the morning of the first day of the program.[3] In addition to lending credibility to the orientation program, we believed that the exam would be helpful for a number of other reasons. First, the examination would provide background information on students, especially in cases where TOEFL scores were not available. Second, it would help in determining whether we could proceed with the program as planned. Third, it would provide information to assist in limiting enrollment in the event that there were too many students. Finally, we felt it might serve UCI administrators in assessing needs for the ongoing program.

## General Overview of the Program

With the exception of the first day, which included the administration of the ESLPE and a campus tour in the morning, the program consisted of five afternoons of approximately four hours of instruction per day. Each day's activities were varied as much as possible by alternating types of activities and modes of instruction. There were approximately three breaks per afternoon, one of which was extended to include refreshments. A schedule of the program is presented below:

We should note here that we were greatly assisted by the staff of the Learning Skills Center. They were present in the classroom as observers and aides, and did much to alleviate the tasks of classroom management. Since the Learning Skills Center staff were to be responsible for the second, ongoing phase of TA training, their involvement in the orientation afforded them the opportunity to get to know the students and thus provide continuity between the two phases of the program.

## Administrative Sessions

On the first and last days of the program, there were several sessions which focused on administrative matters. The first afternoon session began with a presentation by the foreign student adviser regarding such matters as immigration and housing. Following this presentation, there was a general introductory session during which we distributed schedules for the week and explained the program objectives. During the last session on Friday, students were asked to evaluate the week-long program.

| MONDAY | TUESDAY | WEDNESDAY | THURSDAY | FRIDAY |
|---|---|---|---|---|
| 1:00 Immigration Information | 1:00 Introduction to the Checklist | 1:00 Note-taking | 1:00 University Lecture 1: Political Geography | 1:00 Seeing Yourself on Videotape 3 |
| 1:30 Welcome and Introductions | | | | |
| 2:30 Break | 2:00 Organization Workshop | 2:00 Seeing Your-self on Videotape 2 | 2:00 Practice Essay Test | 2:30 Break |
| 2:45 Seeing Your-self on Videotape 1 | 2:50 Break | 3:20 Break | 2:50 Break | 2:40 University Lecture 2: Western Civilization |
| | 3:10 Presentation Workshop | | 3:10 Cultural Panel | Practice Objective Test |
| 3:45 Student Teacher Problem Solving Exercise | 4:00 Instructor Model Presentation | 3:40 Focus on Question Formation | 4:00 Cultural Problem Solving Exercise | 4:00 Evaluations and Happy Hour |

Figure 1.  Schedule for one-week training program for foreign teaching assistants. (Arrows indicate concurrent sessions during which the students were divided into two groups and taught separately. All other sessions were team taught.)

## Student VTR Presentations

As suggested above, the extensive use of videotaping provided the focal point of the orientation program. By way of clarification, we should note that the videotape recording was used in two different kinds of activities. In one, student presentations were recorded and played back; and in the other, videotapes of university lectures were used to provide practice in listening and note-taking.

The first of these activities, the student VTR presentations, was intended to provide the students with an opportunity to see themselves on videotape and to help them determine where they needed improvement in making oral presentations. During the week-long orientation program, student presentations were taped and played back on the first, third, and fifth days.

The first student taping session was designed to familiarize the participants with the procedure. Students were asked to choose from a list of topics and give an impromptu one-minute talk.[4] The list included topics such as "My initial impressions of the U.S." and "My major field and why I chose it." Following the taping of student presentations, the recordings were played back and students were given an opportunity to react to their own presentations. Additional comments were kept to a minimum on the first day since the emphasis was more on familiarizing the participants with the presentation and taping procedure than on evaluation.

On the second day of the program, four sessions were conducted to help prepare students for the subsequent VTR presentations. These included an introduction to the evaluation checklist (see Appendix A), an organization workshop, a presentation workshop, and two demonstration presentations by the course instructors. While the organization workshop stressed the importance of carefully planning a presentation, the proper use of visual aids and kinesics was emphasized in the presentation workshop. Both workshops were conducted informally and students were encouraged to take a major role in the discussions.

The introduction to the evaluation checklist involved a discussion and clarification of each evaluative category. Then, using the checklist, students evaluated a short, well-delivered videotaped lecture. After completing the checklist, students discussed their ratings and the rationale for each.

In the fourth preparatory session, we attempted to review the major points presented in the organization and presentation workshops. To demonstrate what would be required of students in their VTR presentations, we took a concept from our own field, the difference between a phoneme and a morpheme. One instructor provided the students with a model of "what to do" by presenting the difference as clearly and effectively as possible; the other instructor provided a model of "what not to do." The latter presentation was characterized by distracting gestures, heavy dependence on notes, and a lack of visual aids. During these demonstrations, students had two additional opportunities to use the evaluation checklist.

For the second and third VTR sessions, students were asked to present a three-minute explanation of a concept from their major field. Using the checklist, the instructor and students evaluated each speaker's presentation. Before the floor was opened to group critique, the videotaped presentations were played back, and the presenters were invited to comment on their own performances. Following this self-evaluation, other students had the opportunity to make comments before giving the presenter the completed checklist.

## Note-taking and Test-taking Experience

The second VTR component, the video-recorded university lectures, provided the students with note-taking and test-taking practice. Whereas the VTR student presentations discussed above were aimed more at the skills that a TA might need, the note-taking and test-taking experiences attempted to provide a preview of parts of American academic life which would be especially relevant to the newly arrived foreign student.

VTR lectures were used on three different occasions. The first lecture was a simulated humanities lecture which had been prepared for note-taking practice in advanced ESL classes at UCLA. Students were given partially completed notes and were told to fill in what was missing. Following the exercise, we asked students to share what they had written to verify that they had comprehended the major points of the lecture. The second two recordings were of actual college lectures in political geography and history. For these, students were required to take notes on their own. Following the geography lecture, we gave the students sample essay questions and time to prepare answers in study groups. They were then given an essay question based on the lecture and were allowed fifteen minutes to organize and write their responses. The history lecture was followed by a multiple choice test, which was provided to give students practice with another mode of testing.

## Communication Exercises

As we have noted above, students had frequent opportunities for group work in class. While group work was incidentally incorportated into a number of activities, two sessions focused solely on group interaction. The first of these was a problem-solving and role-playing exercise involving such issues as grading, cheating, and plagiarism. The second session was an adaptation of a Values Clarification (Simon, Howe, and Kirschenbaum, 1972) exercise concerning foreign students' attitudes toward Americans. This session followed a cultural panel during which the students related their problems of acculturating to American life.

## Program Evaluation

On the last day, students were given an opportunity to evaluate the program. We asked them to rate each session on a scale of 0 to 5; and for each session, we provided space for additional comments. Because there were several other conflicting activities which students were obliged to attend during orientation week, and attendance was more or less optional, the number of students present fluctuated. Of the twenty-six students on our original roster, an average of twenty attended daily. Sixteen of these students completed the program evaluation. Results of the evaluation are presented in Table 1.

Ratings on the six-point scale ranged from a high of 4.79 to a low of 3.11. The VTR student presentations received the highest ratings (4.79 for sessions two and three, and 4.77 for the preliminary session). Next highest were the practice objective test (4.58), the instructors' demonstration presentations (4.55), and the cultural panel (4.50). In descending order, lowest ratings were given to the session on question formation (3.71), the two communication exercises (3.67 and 3.64) and the campus tour (3.11).

In their written comments, most of the students praised the program. They expressed their approval of the program's focus on global communication skills rather than on discrete points of language. Repeatedly, students emphasized the value of seeing themselves on videotape and of getting to know other foreign

Table 1. *Results of student evaluations of the one-week orientation program*

| Session | Mean | Number |
|---|---|---|
| 1. Student VTR presentation 2 | 4.79 | 14 |
| 2. Student VTR presentation 3 | 4.79 | 14 |
| 3. Student VTR presentation 1 | 4.77 | 13 |
| 4. Practice objective test | 4.58 | 12 |
| 5. Instructor demonstration presentations | 4.55 | 11 |
| 6. Cultural panel | 4.50 | 12 |
| 7. Note-taking | 4.43 | 14 |
| 8. Immigration information | 4.23 | 13 |
| 9. Presentation workshop | 4.10 | 11 |
| 10. Introduction to checklist | 3.92 | 12 |
| 11. University lecture 2 | 3.92 | 12 |
| 12. University lecture 1 | 3.91 | 11 |
| 13. Practice essay test | 3.91 | 11 |
| 14. Organization workshop | 3.83 | 12 |
| 15. Focus on question formation | 3.71 | 14 |
| 16. Cultural problem solving exercise | 3.67 | 12 |
| 17. Student/teacher problem solving exercise | 3.64 | 14 |
| 18. Campus tour | 3.11 | 9 |

*Students ranked the above sessions on a scale of 0 to 5. Sixteen students ($N = 16$) completed evaluation forms. The figures in the Number column represent the number of students who participated in a session.

students. Several of them acknowledged their gratitude to the university for setting up the program.

The major criticism of the program had to do with time factors. Some students complained that the program was too concentrated and that the breaks were not long enough, and others recommended that the program be spread out over a longer period of time. It was also suggested that the program start earlier so that students would have more time before school began. As it was, the program ended on Friday and regular classes began on the following Monday.

## Instructor Reactions

In response to the student evaluations, we would like to add some of our own reactions. First, we too feel that the VTR student presentations were the most valuable aspect of the program; however, we fear that some of the students gave the activity a high rating for the wrong reasons. Although some students were well prepared and utilized the experience to its fullest, others were unprepared and failed to attend to the content and organization of their presentations. In short, the overall quality of the student VTR presentations was not as high as we had hoped, and we feel that the student ratings reflect more the superficial thrill of seeing oneself on videotape than an objective evaluation of its instructional value.

Second, it is interesting to note that student ratings of communication activities were among the lowest, and yet in our opinion these were some of the liveliest and most popular activities. By way of explanation, we believe that many foreign students tend to place more value on teacher-centered instruction than on peer interaction/instruction. In view of our own positive evaluation of these activities, the opportunities they provided for socialization, and their relatively high ratings (3.67 and 3.64), we would still include communication exercises in any similar program.

Although we feel that the orientation program was a success, we do not wish to delude ourselves about how much the students "learned" in one week. While we attempted to expose the participants to some ideas and skills which might help them in their academic careers as students and TAs, we feel that the most positive aspects of the orientation were the possibilities provided for students to get acquainted with other foreign students and with various offices and individuals on campus. Thus, in our opinion, the advantages of a one-week orientation program exist more in the realm of affect than in that of learning and instruction.

## Conclusion

In closing, we would like to offer several suggestions for administrators who are considering the establishment of special programs for foreign TAs and/

or foreign students. We think it is important that administrators carefully consider the objectives of any special program and limit them according to the time available for instruction. If, for example, the aim of the program is to familiarize students with the campus and with certain aspects of university life, then a one-week program may well be appropriate. More time will obviously be needed, however, if the program aims at improving TA intelligibility or at improving the study skills of foreign students.

In addition to specifying the nature of the program, we feel that it is equally important to specify the population of students for whom the program is intended. Criteria should be established to determine who should attend the classes and, if necessary, on what basis enrollment should be limited. In this regard, consideration may need to be given to such factors as test scores, previous grades, and departmental referrals. Additionally, a decision should be made as to whether attendance is required or optional.

Finally, the scheduling of special programs merits the support and cooperation of the entire university community. In being asked to attend these programs, foreign students should not be isolated from the mainstream of campus life. Thus, inter-departmental efforts should be made to schedule such programs at times which are least likely to conflict with other campus activities. If programs for foreign students are deemed important, then they should be scheduled at times which allow students to attend and at the same time do not deprive them of the opportunity to participate in other orientation programs where they can meet with their native-speaking peers.

## Endnotes

1. This chapter was originally presented at the Annual CATESOL State Conference in Los Angeles in 1979. It first appeared in J. Povey (ed.)., 1979, Workspapers in Teaching English as a Second Language, Vol. 13, pp. 49-68, University of California, Los Angeles. We wish to acknowledge our appreciation to Frances Hinofotis, Kathleen Bailey, and Susan Stern for many of the ideas we implemented in the program discussed in this chapter.

2. Though determined solely on the basis of the instructors' intuitions of students' academic needs, the above list exhibits a high degree of similarity to students' own perceptions of their needs, as determined by a survey of UCLA students, reported in Bailey (1977).

3. We wish to thank Dr. Earl Rand for his cooperation in providing us with UCLA's English as a Second Language Placement Exam.

4. For lists of possible topics, see the appendices to the chapters by Rice, and by Bailey and Hinofotis, both in this volume.

# A One-semester Program
## for Orienting the New Foreign Teaching Assistant[1]

### DONNA STEED RICE

*T*he subject of internationalizing higher education is a topic of current interest in the academic community. At a conference dedicated to the problems and possibilities for internationalizing higher education, Dr. Burton Clark, Director of the Yale University Higher Education Research Group, stated that, "In the last two decades, Americans have been looking more and more to the work of foreign researchers in various disciplines." From this observation we can conclude that, if the concept of international education is to be developed, we can expect a significant increase in the international exchange of scholars in the future, and thus, in all probability, an increase in the number of foreign teaching assistants in U.S. university classrooms.

The rationale for this chapter lies in the belief that if institutions of higher learning are truly committed to the concept of international education, then they have a moral as well as an academic obligation to familiarize the foreign teaching assistant with the sociocultural and academic differences in the university system that may cause communication breakdowns within the classroom.

## Course Goals and Activities

This chapter focuses on the content and evaluation of an orientation program which was developed for new foreign TAs at the Intensive English Language Institute of the State University of New York at Buffalo in order to meet the following objectives:

1. To improve the oral/aural proficiency and reading/writing skills of the non-native speaking TA, both in the classroom and in the pursuance of graduate studies;

2. To perfect classroom teaching and interaction techniques that are appropriate to the U.S. university classroom;

3. To provide an understanding of the educational and philosophical bases for the U.S. university graduate and undergraduate curricula;

4. To teach the foreign TA to anticipate, through interaction activities and role-playing, the types of situations that are likely to be encountered in the U.S. classroom;

5. To enable foreign teaching assistants to understand the respective roles of the faculty and TAs, the university administrative procedures which affect the foreign TA, matters of grading and testing, and the general communications network of the university community.

The chapter discusses the organization of the program, describes some of the techniques used to accomplish the intended goals, and offers suggestions for the planning of future programs of this type.

The pilot project for this training program was begun in September of 1978. It consisted of one weekly two-hour session for thirteen weeks. Enrollment was voluntary. Total enrollment ranged from sixteen to twenty-two students, representing ten languages and various disciplines, including operative dentistry, mathematics, oral medicine, political science, engineering, physics, English literature, computer science, and microbiology. TOEFL scores of the group ranged from 449 to 632. No required text was used, but students were referred to McKeachie's classic Teaching tips: A guidebook for beginning teachers (1978). The scope of the course was intentionally broad, and was designed to include three major components: (1) oral/aural English, (2) reading and writing, and (3) cross-cultural orientation to the U.S. university system and communication network.

The first session of the course, a general orientation to higher education in the United States, proved to be one of the most valuable in terms of needs assessment. The session consisted of a brief overview of the history and philosophy of higher education in the U.S. and an open forum on problems of both an institutional and administrative nature which the foreign TAs themselves perceived to be significant. It soon became quite apparent that although the foreign TAs were university students, they had come to this country as graduates and had little or no knowledge of American undergraduate curricula in terms of distribution requirements, university policy, grading, and general classroom procedures. Local acronyms, such as DUE (Division of Undergraduate Education), were meaningless to them. In other words, they lacked a basis for understanding the teaching situation in which they had been placed. For example, they could not understand what they perceived to be the "apathetic attitudes" of some of their students toward the subject matter. Foreign TAs in the sciences related that they had expected to find a classroom filled with dedicated future scientists, rather than a class composed of *some* majoring students and others who were merely fulfilling distribution requirements. Like-wise, they did not understand the almost aggressive "attacks" by some students who received a grade of B + on a report rather than an A.

As a result of information gained from an informal needs assessment conducted in the first session, we found it necessary to modify the previously planned syllabus somewhat in order to increase its effectiveness. The syllabus had been designed according to what we thought the TAs' needs would be. However, the needs analysis results made it apparent that the foreign TAs had many concerns which had to be addressed immediately. Most of the modifi-cations involved the sequencing of materials in the various components (e.g., an earlier and greater emphasis on cross-cultural communication problems), rather than changes in actual course content. However, the requirement for the course participants to write a research paper was dropped, although the concept was discussed thoroughly.

## The Oral/Aural Component

The objectives of the first component, the oral/aural segment, were to develop the comprehension and communication skills of the foreign TAs both as teachers and as students. In this respect, the goal was not only the mastery of the linguistic features of the language needed for oral production, but also to help the non-native speaking TAs understand why students complained of being unable to understand them, and conversely, why they had difficulty understanding their professors' lectures and directions. Teaching assistants from India, for example, had spoken English since childhood, but were still virtually unintelligible to Americans because of differences in stress, intonation, rhythm, etc.

Listening and speaking problems caused particular difficulties in some typical college classroom activities. For the new foreign TAs and for some of the more experienced ones, such concepts as brainstorming and the oral report were clearly a source of trauma. Special attention was given to these issues. Techniques for increasing listening comprehension, such as listening for cause/effect relationships, were practiced.

As the project developed, it became increasingly apparent that many of the foreign TAs' problems in the classroom were not directly language related. Problems such as maintaining classroom discipline and not being able to respond "on the spot" to both legitimate questions and to those questions that were not entirely academic in scope were high on the priority list for class discussion. We dealt with the problem of spontaneous response through the use of impro-visations and role-playing flavored with a bit of humor. (See Appendix A for a list of improvisation topics). In very little time, the group became quite adept at fielding some of these types of questions.

In terms of classroom discipline, an effort was made to help the participants become more aware of classroom related sociocultural differences that affect the learning situation. A unit on "how to disagree politely" was incorporated as an on-going part of the course. The foreign TAs practiced phrases such as the following:

> "I understand your point of view; however, it has been my experience that . . . . "
> "Your point is well taken; however, I would argue that. . . . "
> "That's a good point, but do you think that . . . ?" "Hmm, I never thought of that. Still. . . . "

Such phrases were useful for the TAs in both their roles—as graduate students and as teachers.

Also discussed were the use of body language to maintain class order and ways of dealing with the student who asks the rhetorical question that may be designed merely to test the teacher's patience or skill, rather than to seek information. Conversely, foreign TAs were taught how to read the students' body language in order to determine their own effectiveness as teachers. Since most of the group had had little or no teaching experience prior to their TA assignments, they were most grateful for such teaching tips.

To introduce the unit on body language, the silent Charlie Chaplin film, "The Immigrant," was shown. It illustrated that people do indeed communicate without using words. After viewing the film, the participants discussed what the foreign TAs themselves do with their bodies when they are bored, tired, or disinterested in a classroom. Information was provided on the theories of Birdwhistle (1971) and Knapp (1972) about kinesics, the utilization of classroom space, and seating arrangements for small groups.

At the next class meeting, a film about an American high school classroom was shown. It was a segment of the old television series "Room 222" entitled "Funny Money." Prior to viewing the film, the TAs in the training program observed both students' and teachers' body language and classroom behavior in general. The film has excellent examples of facial expressions and body language which suggest dogmatism, defensiveness, and boredom. The TAs analyzed the film for instances of each.

## The Reading and Writing Component

The objectives of the second component, reading and writing, again were directed toward skills needed for both successful teaching and successful graduate study. Techniques for increasing reading speed and overall comprehension of academic and periodical literature, discussion of the recognition and use of appropriate levels of diction, and appropriate reasoning and argumentation in the academic term paper were addressed. Some thought was also given to the types of learning that could be anticipated within the context of the U.S. university system (i.e., a preference in many disciplines for synthesized critical understanding of concepts versus the rote memorization of facts) and the role of the teacher in facilitating such learning.

The assignment and assessment of a library research paper were identified as matters of grave concern to the group. One of the more heated discussions of the semester centered on the question of whether or not foreign TAs should be expected to grade students for their grammar and writing skills, as some native-speaking TAs tend to do. Because of many extenuating circumstances, this question remained unresolved, but the general consensus of the group regarding such corrections was negative.

Although program funding was limited for anything other than the course instructor, every effort was made to acquaint the foreign TAs with all aspects of classroom instruction, since many of them had had no training as teachers. On-campus expertise was used in special areas when possible. For example, an educational psychologist lectured on testing and evaluation. An introduction to the use and availability of on-campus audiovisual equipment was also presented by a specialist in media studies. These presentations were well received by the foreign TAs and eased the ESL teacher's burden of preparation.

## The Cross-Cultural Component

The third component of the project dealt with a cross-cultural orientation to the U.S. university system. This component consisted of three two-part modules, which out of necessity were dispersed at intervals throughout the course. The first module, models of education in the U.S., was divided into two meetings. One was presented as part of the general orientation. The other was introduced later and involved a lecture/discussion about the absence of a centralized educational governing body to standardize procedures in this country and how this lack affects the concept of academic freedom.

The effects of the "publish or perish syndrome" on the foreign TA also proved to be of interest. In the medical and scientific fields in particular, the foreign TAs were often asked to present papers at both on- and off-campus conferences, or were encouraged to submit papers to journals. Even though many of the TAs had published in their own countries, they were reluctant to do so in English and wanted to know what would happen if they refused. Thus the TA course provided clarification about publishing and presenting in hopes of minimizing the fear associated with these activities.

The second module was entitled study skills and administrative procedures. It dealt with the manner in which students approached their instructors, student expectations in terms of teacher availability, and the importance of the immediate "grade" in terms of future departmental admissions.

The content of the third module, a cross-cultural seminar which had been planned for the end of the course, became interwoven as an on-going orientation throughout the semester. This change was a direct result of the informal needs analysis conducted at the first class meeting.

On the whole, the staff and the students involved in this particular program agreed that its goals and objectives had been satisfied. This conclusion is based on the results of an informal questionnaire. In addition, in casual discussions with the instructor, the foreign TAs themselves reported that they were more confident in the classroom.

## Planning Future Programs

However, there are a few considerations to which future planners of programs of this type should give serious thought. When one reads the criticism of foreign teaching assistants voiced by American students in the media, the hidden assumption appears to be that, if one can teach non-native speaking TAs to master the production of oral English, then an increase in the quality of teaching will be automatically followed by increased understanding and learning in the foreign TAs' classrooms. Nevertheless, it is common knowledge that perfect oral English skills do not necessarily make a good teacher.

Many of the foreign TAs' problems are related to sociocultural differences and poor instructional methodology as well as to lack of linguistic skills. In fact, whether American students who complain so strongly about not being able to "understand" the foreign TAs would be able to "understand" a native speaker any better, given that language were the only denominator, and whether or not the student is unknowingly reacting to sociocultural differences as well as to linguistic variables, remains an unanswered question.

This is *not* to say that being able to speak the language is not an important prerequisite for intelligibility in the classroom. Such an assumption would be naive to the point of absurdity. However, when designing an orientation course for foreign TAs, the true weight of accent-free English is worthy of accurate assessment in terms of determining goals, objectives and curriculum content. It is likely that foreign TAs who are 95 percent unintelligible at the beginning of a one-semester training program will in all probability be 75 percent unintelligible at the end of the course, regardless of the content, unless the course is very intensive. It would seem much more logical then, that people who have the necessary TOEFL scores and academic qualifications, but who lack the oral English skills for teaching, be directed into non-teaching kinds of assistantships rather than be placed in a classroom situation where they can be predicted to perform poorly.

In terms of motivation for enrollment in such courses, the element of time must be considered. Most TAs will be graduate students for a limited number of years—usually two or three. Since most foreign TAs face heavy graduate study demands as well as their teaching schedules, it is unreasonable to expect that they will volunteer to spend more than a minimum number of hours in a training program once the semester begins. The question then becomes "What kind of course can one design in order to meet the greatest need in a limited amount of time?"

For graduate students planning to return to their native countries immediately upon completion of the degree program, there will be even less incentive to improve their teaching skills in English. The solution, in terms of motivation, may well be to provide an intensive orientation which focuses on all aspects of classroom instruction *prior* to the undertaking of the teaching assignment. (For a discussion of such programs, see the chapters by Gaskill and Brinton, and by Shaw and Garate, both in this volume.) Such an alternative would provide new foreign TAs with the information about the university system, sociocultural differences and teaching methods *before* rather than after they become involved in a teaching situation. Such an alternative would also allow time for reassignment if it were discovered that a selected teaching assistant was incapable of teaching. Granted, there are many problems which can be foreseen as being inherent in such a plan, but once the commitment to international education is made, some steps must be taken to ensure academic excellence in the teaching done by foreign TAs.

## Endnotes

1. This chapter is a revised version of a paper presented at the 31st Annual Conference of NAFSA in Phoenix, Arizona, May 9, 1979.

Appendix A. *Improvisations for foreign TA training*
1. You are a TA. You have been late for class several times. On one particular day when you arrive, you are surprised to find the professor for whom you work waiting for you. He is very angry. Convince him that you are not irresponsible and that you have a legitimate excuse. (5 minutes)
2. You are a TA. You have told the students that they must buy a certain text which costs $25.00. They protest. Convince them that this is the most important book written in this field in the 20th century and that they must have it on Monday. (2 minutes)
3. You are an instructor. You have just given a student his grade. He thinks he deserves an A. You gave him a D. Convince the student that you are right and he is wrong. (5 minutes)
4. You are an instructor. You have explicitly given the directions for an assignment. On the date that the assignment is due, one student says, "But teacher, I didn't understand the assignment so I didn't do it!" Respond to him very politely, but firmly. Give him a deadline or a negative alternative if he doesn't do the assignment. (2 minutes)
5. You are an instructor. Your students want to know if you give pop quizzes, make-ups, standardized tests, open book exams, hourlies, and departmental exams. Explain your philosophy on testing to the students. (2 minutes)
6. You are an instructor. You have just announced a quiz for Friday. Several students ask, "What is it going to be about?" "How long is the test?" " What kind of test is it?" "What should we study?" Explain to the students that the test questions will be taken right from the book (but do not use the word book), that they will select (a), (b), or (c) as the correct answer (but do not say (a), (b), or (c).) Answer all of their questions in less than two minutes.
7. You are an instructor. One of your students made you so angry that *you hit the roof,* felt that you had *had it up to here, gave him fair warning,* and told him that he had better be *up to his ears in studying* if he expects to pass. Say all of these things in a very *polite,* but emphatic, manner!

# Problems and Strategies:
## An Extended Training Program for Foreign Teaching Assistants

JEAN ZUKOWSKI/FAUST

*T*o their American students foreign TAs in the University of Arizona's chemistry department were having a "pronunciation problem." The Americans wrote in their course evaluations that they could not understand the directions that they were given by the foreign TAs, that the foreign TAs were not able to explain problems very well, and that—in some cases—they did not believe that the foreign TAs knew the field of chemistry well enough to teach it. Because the chemistry department staffs most undergraduate courses with teaching assistants, a significant number of whom were foreign TAs, a decision was made to organize a special spoken English class for them, one that would address the special "pronunciation difficulties" that their students perceived.[1]

## The Analysis

Informal evaluations of the English of the eight foreign TAs conducted by the course instructor showed these results:

1. All eight spoke English well enough to carry on comfortable, mutually intelligible conversations with a native speaker about their backgrounds, about current world happenings, and even about the problems they were having in their classrooms.

2. All eight were able to understand each other in ordinary conversations, according to the judgment of the class participants, their supervisors, and the teacher of the class.

3. All eight were able to write well enough in English to be placed in

advanced composition classes or to warrant exemption from further study of English, as evaluated by the University of Arizona's Test of American English Rhetoric.

Obviously, from the fact that all had been successfully engaged in graduate study for at least a year, these foreign TAs were capable of understanding the English language as used in advanced chemistry study.

What then was their problem? For diagnostic purposes the foreign TAs were asked to prepare a simple explanation of a chemical process or a laboratory procedure to present in class, such as how to operate a centrifuge or what happens when salt is added to an already saturated solution. The assignment was intended to be related to their graduate work and yet similar to the kind of presentation that foreign TAs are expected to give to their students; it was intended to be something that anyone could understand.

It was during these simple presentations that the problems began to emerge. It seemed that there was a connection between the familiarity of the audience with the topic and the success of the communication. Therefore, a second oral assignment was made: the chemistry TAs, who were all students in one advanced seminar and were therefore all at the same level of accomplishment in chemistry, were asked to prepare the theoretical problems that they were working on in their own research for oral presentation to the class.

In this assignment, it was assumed that their English teacher would understand the language but not the chemistry involved, and that the other foreign TAs would be able to understand both. The focus was to be whether the English was understandable. It was not understandable to either the chemists or to the English teacher—in fact, the English seemed to deteriorate quickly as the chemistry became more complex. In other words, as the subject became less familiar and less common, the listeners were much more likely to have trouble understanding. The words seemed to slur; the discourse seemed to become monotone.

Yet only part of the problem lay in the linguistic competence of the foreign TAs; their "pronunciation" was good enough when the linguistic domain was clearly defined (e.g., the language used in talking about one's background) but not so in less familiar discussions. Tape recordings proved that their scholarly presentations were no more monotonous than the more personal presentations had been. The listener, it seemed, was providing much of the comprehensibility to those conversations. When the listener was not able to contribute to the comprehension, the pronunciation of the foreign TA was blamed and the speech seemed to become less animated.[2]

## The Strategies

To determine the roots of the foreign TAs' spoken language problems, the class members brainstormed about the reasons why they were having difficulties. The following observations on the foreign TAs' language and linguistic situation were synthesized and recognized as basic to their problems:

1. Technical words are often the same in both their native languages and English.
2. Chemistry involves an international symbolic language in the same way that mathematics does.
3. The more advanced one is in graduate study, the more likely one is to use jargon and "in-expressions," language that an undergraduate could not be expected to understand in English and that a non-native speaker might not recognize as extra-ordinary expressions for the concept.

Thus foreign TAs must learn not to rely solely on technical jargon in community with their students. Bailey points out that the native speakers of any language encourage a person learning their language to use colloquialisms, "but 'book-ishness' comes closer to what foreigners are taught as 'correct' English . . . " (Bailey 1978, 230). The implications for the foreign TAs entail a double bind; they must speak one way to be accepted by their peers and professors, and another way to be understood by their students. Unfortunately, they have few opportunities to learn the difference between the two "languages" they are to speak. Furthermore, there are few if any written authorities to tell them which is which and how to use the two levels of language.

The implications of these observations about their language situation were meaningful to the FTAs. They expressed both surprise that their discussion had resulted in concrete ideas about why they were having communication problems in their classes (awareness of the problem) and hope that they might be able to correct it (a commitment to the class work).

Because the chemistry terminology was already familiar to these graduate chemists in their own language, the foreign TAs had made little attempt to pronounce the words within the English phonological system. As a result, their undergraduate students were mystified as to what "so diem cried" (sodium chloride) meant, what "ennetch-three" (NH3) was for, what the importance of a "green frask" (clean flask) was, and what made a "neat-leet" (nitrite). Furthermore, because the foreign TAs were transferring whole sets of words from one language to another, the overhang of the native language phonology also affected the other English words in the immediate environment, making their English even more foreign-sounding.

Because of the international symbolic language of chemistry, the foreign TAs felt comfortable in using the oral equivalents of the written shorthand, a practice that American chemistry teachers used far less frequently and one that mystified their American students all the more. (For example, a foreign TA might say "enay-o-etch pruss etch-see-air equals etch-two-woe pruss enay-see-air" instead of "sodium hydroxide plus hydrochloric acid equals water plus sodium chloride.")

Because all of English is foreign to the TAs, the "in-expressions" of chemistry used by their American peers were no more foreign to them than ordinary discourse. They quickly adopted the conversational style and jargon of the American graduate teaching assistants in an effort to be accepted, for a group is bound by such in-expressions (Weinberg 1979, 55). However, because the foreign TAs were not sensitive to the change in language level that the jargon signified, they used it freely in freshman classes. Their students could not understand it; they would not have understood it from a native speaker, but the native-speaking TAs understood the language level difference.[3]

The list of observations just discussed resulted from the course instructor's interaction with the foreign TAs and from their own discussions of the problem. The implications of these observations about their language situation were meaningful to the foreign TAs. They expressed both surprise that their discussion had resulted in "concrete" ideas of why they were having communication problems in their classes (awareness of the problem) and hope that they might be able to correct it (a commitment to the class work). The strategies that resulted from the observations began at the word level, progressed to sentence level, to organization, and then to paralanguage.

## The Sounds and Rhythms of English

The first step in convincing the foreign TAs that their native language used a different set of sounds was to have them pronounce their own names using English sounds and rhythm. This step was also designed to narrow the perceived distance between a foreign TA and his or her American students, people who would feel more comfortable if they could hear their teacher's name in familiar sounds and would therefore be able to say it. For example, the Arabic pronunciation of "Mahmud" requires the strong pronunciation of the *h* in the middle of the name. Without that *h*, the name seems much easier to pronounce in English.

The foreign TAs' initial resistance was strong, but the ultimate results were positive. They were reluctant to mispronounce their names deliberately, but once they heard how "American" it sounded to do so, they moved, in a sense, away from their traditional language sound patterns, and were able to use English sounds more naturally.

The second step showed that the pronunciation of word syllables followed patterns in English words so that, by analogy with known words, even the most intimidating lexical items could be figured out. A systematic presentation of some common "long" word stress patterns unlocked the secret. For example,

-*ation* as in familiar words like *information, population,* and *nation* was practiced with less common words such as *distillation, procrastination, hyperactivation, condensation, configuration, incorporation, dissertation, obfuscation, electrification,* and *gasification.*

The suffix -*ology,* as in *psychology* and *sociology,* has the same stress pattern in *microbiology, seismology,* and *endocrinology.*

Furthermore, -oscopy follows the pattern of stress movement of the syllable preceding the suffix as in *teloscopy* or *microscopy* or *perioscopy*.

Ferguson (1978, 342), in discussing an instrument for evaluating speaking ability, says that one-word encoding is the kernel for generating "stress-groups," the phrasal units composed of one single stressed syllable together with any unstressed syllables around it. In other words, the way a person breaks up one word affects the stress group that the word occurs in, thereby affecting the whole utterance. If the head word (and a long uncommon word is the most likely element in a phrase to be the head word) is mispronounced, then the whole phrase—if not the whole utterance—is likely to be misunderstood.

For example, if a person intends to say "At the museum I saw an unusual collection of butterflies" and emphasizes *coll-* rather than *-lect-* of the phrasal object, the hearer will probably process the "At the museum I saw . . . " part of the message, but not the object phrase. This blurring of other environmental segments is probably due in part to the resulting distortion of intonation, and in part to the confusion of the listener's expectations.

## Sentence-level Strategies

Next the class reviewed the basic intonation patterns of English, including statements, question-word questions, yes-no questions, emphasis, calling and naming. These basic sentence intonation patterns were applied with the principle of emphasis and contrast (Sledd 1959, 22-29), in which the students were asked to stress first the head words and then the contrasted elements to reinforce the use of the emphasis. The net result was a greater break between words (juncture), an effect which made the individual words more easily comprehensible, broke up the steady speech rhythm, and destroyed the monotone—all resulting in clearer, more enthusiastic delivery (Lado 1957, 40-41, 148). For example, the students began with sentences like this:

Don't take the *big* one, take the *small* one.

They progressed to sentences like this:

When the water is *blue*, you know there is probably *copper* in it. When the compound is *red*, there is probably *iron* in it.

## Organizational Strategies

Next the class studied the principle of redundancy in lectures. In general their training in English rhetoric and organization had come indirectly through reading and more directly through instruction in composition, both areas of English expression in which conciseness and parsimony are highly valued (Kaplan 1966). The natural outcome of learning a foreign rhetoric and superimposing it on a more naturally acquired method of development and then practicing it (and doing so well, as evidenced by their advanced composition placement) was an unwitting emphasis on tight construction of thought organization. The tight construction and parsimony were reflected in their oral presentations: The foreign TAs were likely to state each idea, including the topic sentence, only once. For example, one foreign TA's report on an unusual invention began as follows:

> I have seen a methane-powered car in Modesto, California. It is revolutionary in design. The city officials are sponsoring the project. Garbage at the city dump . . .

A more natural lecture style includes internal references and repetition of concepts:

> I have seen a methane-powered car in Modesto, California. The city officials of this central California town, being concerned about fossil fuel consumption, are sponsoring this revolutionary project, one which would utilize methane, the gas produced by garbage, to run an automobile. By converting the garbage at the Modesto city dump into methane for fuel. . . .

In the redundant model, the listener has far more opportunity to catch any information that might have been missed the first time around. Therefore, because the foreign TAs were less likely to repeat parts of their sentences, it seemed to the American undergraduates that they had little to say about the subject, that it was "hard to follow them," and that the foreign TAs did not know enough chemistry to teach. Added to the problems that the students were having in understanding the concepts of chemistry and the accented language of the non-native speakers, this diversion from the expected lecture delivery style made their language almost as foreign as French would have been.

In a group discussion at the outset of the foreign TA course, one of the unhappy foreign TAs had interpreted the situation as simply a problem with students having to take chemistry to meet general university science requirements. "They don't like chemistry and they have to take it, so they blame us for their problems." The problem, however, is more complex than that.

A second strategy to help make the foreign TAs' concept organization more accessible to the students is the reflective listening technique. If a person wants to be sure to be in complete communication with another, he or she repeats the ideas (not the words) that are questioned (Gordon 1973, 49-94). For example, when a student asks a question, the teacher should rephrase the question as he or she repeats it. This repetition serves both to frame the subsequent answers for the rest of the class and to assure the student who asked the question that it has been understood and is about to be answered.

The effect of non-rephrasal of a question is at best somewhat unsettling to a student; at its worst, the foreign TA's answer might seem entirely unrelated to the question. Because the verbal interaction began without the foreign TA's repetition (i.e., verbal recognition) of the problem, the students' receiving of the response begins with uncertainty (no reassurance) that the foreign TA understood the question and was therefore in a position to answer it.

This reflective technique serves to increase the communication between every teacher and student. An even more active approach enhances understanding yet further. Called skillful (or active) listening, this technique involves verbally interpreting what the student has asked, relating the question to the larger scope of the course or course unit, and then—after restatement—answering the interpreted question. This sequence of presentation builds rapport between teacher and class; its non-use might hinder communication.

The third organizational strategy involved practicing the use of transitional devices. The foreign TAs had been taught to use phrases such as *for example, for this reason, in the same way,* and *on the other hand,* in their English writing, but for some unknown reason, in the taped oral presentations, they did not use these expressions.[4] The foreign TAs were urged to substitute these English ways of indicating thought pattern instead of other culturally indicated ways of signifying "thinking-on-your-feet" time. The drone of an *ahhh* or *errrr* underscores lack of confidence in English rather than meaning "I am considering an answer" as it does in Japanese, Arabic, and many other languages. Furthermore, transitional phrases cue the students as to what kind of evidence the foreign TA might be offering to answer the question. With a hint that the foreign TA is about to give an example, a reason, an analogy, or a contrast, the listeners can become prepared to contribute part of the form to the answer, that is, to provide a larger part of the comprehension than would have been possible without the clues. In addition, limiting the scope of the answer reduces the anxiety level of the students; the answer is therefore less likely to seem obscure and unrelated, since most miscues would be eliminated.

## Body Language

The last aspect of the classroom communication problem that faced the foreign TAs was how to adapt their total communication to the informal teaching situation, how to project confidence, and how to establish authority in a way that was culturally understandable for American undergraduate students. Essential to this learning is cognition of how body language works. The foreign TAs needed to understand that nonverbal communication functions in the following ways:

1. it supports speech by filling in the missing information;
2. it provides feedback to the listener;
3. it controls the synchronization of a group in communication;
4. it communicates attitudes and emotions;
5. it transmits information about personality (Graham and Argyle 1975, 33).

So powerful a communication tool could not be left misunderstood, particularly since the sending of misinformation is more likely to happen in learning a low-gesture language like English (ibid., 33).

In a cross-cultural approach to body symbolism, Douglas says that

Posture, voice, speed, articulation, tonality, all contribute to meaning. The words alone mean very little. Verbal symbols depend on the speaker manipulating his whole environment to get the meaning across. (Douglas 1975, 85)

Douglas continues that the whole thrust of education has been toward over-emphasis of the verbal channel, to the neglect of the kinesic channels.

Because foreign TAs are likely to have learned body languages that are socially acceptable for their particular sex, age, and status group, they are likely to incorporate signals that are appropriate for verbal expression in their home languages and often incongruent with the English equivalent. Furthermore, because the body languages that accompany spoken languages differ greatly, foreign TAs must be made conscious of the potentials for misunderstanding. If the nonverbal signals the American students perceive are leading them to form incorrect attributional impressions of the foreign TAs, then an analysis of the problems and a plan for resolution are in order.

The basic problem, one that is easy to understand in contrastive terms, seems to be a lack of authoritative signals. In the relatively informal relationships between TAs and students, the trappings of authority have been removed. For example, the type of clothing worn at the University of Arizona is extremely informal, whereas in the foreign TAs' native countries the dress of university teachers may distinguish them from the students. Furthermore, first names are frequently used by American students in addressing their teachers, a practice that suggests familiarity and sometimes even intimacy to foreign TAs. In most cultures, the social rules which indicate that there must be distance between teacher and student limit the use of first names (Hall 1959, 71). In many places, titles are used instead of names. Finally, there are differences in expectations of behavior. For example, friendly banter (which involves a high level of language skill) is part of many American college classrooms as students try to outwit teachers. What American teachers understand as rapport resulting from good teaching (that the students' minds are seeking application of the principles taught), foreign TAs are likely to interpret as lack of respect and evidence that their classroom positions are insecure.

For the foreign TA in the University of Arizona course, being unaware of the nonverbal problem was the greatest hindrance to solving it. The challenge was to find those behaviors that spelled out lack of confidence and lack of authority, interpret the problems, and learn to overcome them. In class discussions the foreign TAs and the teacher identified three problems: the need for eye contact, adjustment in pacing or timing, and adaptation of body movements (including voice).

The principle of eye contact, once explained, was easily accepted by the foreign TAs. They had once felt uneasy because their inability to look their students in the eyes (to confront their American students in the American fashion) seemed to be understood by their students as lack of control over a situation. The foreign TAs found that holding the gaze of two or three people in the audience actually made talking to a group easier.

Adjusting timing in practice teaching sessions seemed to come more naturally once the foreign TAs began to incorporate more chalkboard use and more repetition of concepts in their class deliveries. The foreign TAs had tended to prepare complete lesson plans and deliver them almost word for word from elaborate notes. As a result, their deliveries were quite tense, lacking a balance of ideas and examples. The students, who were unable to grasp the great amount of material the foreign TAs tried to present, experienced a build-up of strain. The deliberate use of the chalkboard forced a pacing in their teaching that seemed much more "natural" to American students. (See Shaw and Garate, this volume for further ideas on blackboard techniques for foreign TAs.)

Appropriate new body movements were a difficult lesson for the foreign TAs to learn. Class members were sent to observe Americans who, according to students' evaluations, were good teachers. However, it seemed that good male models were hard to find. Perhaps because most of the processing of body language is done subconsciously, the assignment, to observe native speakers as they lectured, yielded few useful positive observations. One professor, it was reported with disdain, sat on his desk. Another walked around the room. Yet another gripped the lectern.

While these reports did give a few clues for successful body movements in teaching, a far more successful technique was direct imitation of some of these postures in both natural and exaggerated form. This part of the classwork was amusing as well as enlightening. Perhaps it was because a female teacher was imitating male lecturing style that the great differences in ways of exhibiting a confident, assertive manner became obvious, or perhaps rapport was at last established between the instructor and the foreign TAs. In either case, the foreign TAs all seemed to understand what they needed to do. At this point, they made great changes in their teaching styles, incorporating many of the stances and movements they had observed (while noting the unsuccessful ones) and stored unconsciously in their memories.

Practicing these newly acquired tools was tried in front of the videotape camera. For the foreign TAs, videotaping showed some body movement problems. For example, one person stood almost facing the blackboard, writing everything down as if he thought that no one could understand his words. Another stood straight and still as if she were rooted to the spot and too unsure of herself to take a step. Yet another planted his feet and turned only his torso, as if he were firmly established on a base and could not, would not, should not venture far from his position.

Because the foreign TA in attempting to correct the "errors" in English body language is by definition already apprehensive about his or her communication, videotaping in a teaching situation usually elicits the most anxiety and therefore also the person's most natural fear-related behaviors. Videotaped presentations, in this light, provide the most acceptable material for objective analysis of kinesthetic ambiguities and contradictions. The preliminary use of audiotape for word and sentence intonation work was found to desensitize the foreign TAs somewhat to being video recorded. Use of teaching films, with and without sound, not only offers natural ideal models, but also permits the foreign TAs to talk about kinesics as they prepare themselves for similar analyses by becoming accustomed to discussing the postures and expressions of native-speaking teachers.

A major objection might be made to the teaching of gestures and the like: that the second language speakers will be learning how to act. However, it seems that such is not the case. In a study of cross-cultural nonverbal behavior, Graham and Argyle (1975) found that the simple addition of gestures improves the accuracy of descriptions and that, when the appropriate gestures were not permitted, the person needed more words and used fewer internal references such as *it*, *this*, and *here*. Graham and Argyle also inferred from their study that those subjects with less extra verbal ability would have greater difficulty in conveying concepts (ibid., 38). If foreign TAs do not understand and practice culturally appropriate nonverbal behaviors, they may be put in just this position.

The kind of feedback from students which successful description earns the foreign TA is its own reward. Moreover, in persuasion, it is known that engaging in a behavior leads to a change in a related cognitive state. It is not possible to tell whether attitude changes lead to the observed behaviors, or if once the behaviors are realized, the attitudes follow naturally from the behaviors. In any event, should it matter to the foreign TAs except as assurance that cognition of the situation and their options can precipitate more appropriate body language while speaking English, thereby making them more comprehensible?

The foreign TA faces one more potential problem, that of stereotyping. All foreign TAs are subject to this difficulty. However, a strong, preconceived attack on possible stereotyping can serve to subvert students' misconceptions because differences in judgment (about a person) may be the result of the nonverbal communication cues which are used in impression formation (Gitter, Bloch, and Goldman, 1978, 465). According to Black and Monteverde (1974, reported in Gitter, et al.), people who do not have personal information (or a strong and positive attributional first impression) about a person will tend to judge him or her "according to the stereotype associated with the nonverbal cues." In addition, the target person is invited into interpersonal relationships in such a way as to engender the prejudged kind of behavior, that is, to behave in accordance with McMahan's attributional impression (McMahan 1976, 288). Therefore, a person who uses the body language of a leader is assigned qualities of strength, dynamism, and assertiveness, whereas the non-leader is judged as meek, submissive, quiet. A person who acts like a leader will be reacted to as a leader. One whose behavior suggests he or she is not a leader is apt to be stepped on.

Indeed, a study by Weinberg, Smotroff, and Pecke (1978, 88) shows that leadership of the kind required of a teacher is perceived nonverbally through eye contact, proxemics, and arrangement. The factors that describe a leader are self-confidence (assertiveness and poise), openness (a combination of ability to receive and respond to other group members), information (apparent knowledge and the ability to present the information so that it is accessible to the rest of the group), and persuasion (the ability to affect the members of the group while holding their respect). Furthermore, these dimensions of leadership can be learned.

Thus foreign TAs must be prepared to adopt the perceived behaviors of leadership and to remove themselves from their physical stereotypes, while still maintaining their own identities. A small, demure-appearing Thai woman must free herself from the nonassertive model of the folktale Asian woman. The bespectacled Chinese scholar must show himself to be a master of practical material. The athletic-looking African must demonstrate with finesse his or her intellectual abilities. The Mediterranean and the Middle Easterner must prove capacity for focused, forceful application of theory. By successfully avoiding such stereotypes, foreign TAs can help free American students from their misconceptions. In the spirit of international educational exchange, perhaps this breaking of stereotypes, more than all the subject matter knowledge they impart, is the greatest contribution made by foreign TAs.

## Endnotes

1. Hinofotis and Bailey (1980) report that undergraduates, ESL teachers and TA trainers rating videotapes of potential foreign TAs ranked pronunciation as the most important variable influencing the overall ratings awarded the speakers. Pronunciation is a highly salient speech feature and may be perceived as very important, but several of the strategies discussed in this chapter can minimize such phonological difficulties.

2. This observation parallels a finding in research by Keye (1981), in which undergraduates rated personal-cultural presentations by foreign TAs more highly than subject-matter speeches given by the same TAs.

3. In questionnaire research, Bailey (1982a) found that non-majors rated their foreign TAs significantly more critically than did students who were enrolled in the TAs' own disciplines.

4. Tu (1983) has examined the use of transitional expressions in a discourse analysis of four native speaking physics TAs matched with four foreign TAs in the same department.

# Part III
## *The Progress*

# An Evaluation
## *of a Training Course for Foreign Teaching Assistants*[1]

MARK LANDA
WILLIAM PERRY

S ince the early 1970s a serious problem has arisen, at the University of Minnesota and other U.S. universities, regarding the role of foreign graduate students as teaching assistants. In an age of increasing consumerism and ethnocentrism, foreign TAs have been criticized for not providing the quality of education that American undergraduate students demand. As a result, the credibility of foreign students as effective classroom teachers has been greatly undermined.

University graduate departments, which in the past have had to rely only on scores on written English tests to determine the language proficiency of prospective students, can now get a reliable measure of spoken English by requiring the Test of Spoken English. (See Stansfield and Ballard, this volume.) If graduate students have been offered financial support in the form of classroom teaching assistantships, and if, upon arrival, their command of English does not meet departmental standards, they may be referred to an intensive English program for further training. If the institution offers a special course for foreign TAs, they may receive training directly related to the use of English in the classroom.

The investigation reported on in this chapter evaluates the foreign TA course developed at the University of Minnesota and attempts to isolate the variables affecting the success of foreign TAs in American classrooms. The variables that will be examined include English language proficiency and classroom teaching skills as well as the individual TA's attitude toward his or her role as a teacher at an American university.

## Description of the TA Course

The first course for foreign TAs at the University of Minnesota grew out of a faculty seminar on instructional design. It was initially designed and taught by an ESL instructor from the Linguistics Department. The ten-week course focused on improving the TAs' interactional skills, pronunciation, and listening comprehension. The class met twice a week, and each TA had a weekly tutorial session with the instructor. Videotape feedback was used, but on a very limited basis. When the course was offered for the second and third times, it maintained the primary focus on interactional skills and added a component emphasizing effective teaching skills using extensive videotape feedback. The fourth offering of the course, made possible by a Cooperative Projects Grant from the National Association for Foreign Student Affairs, included three weekly class sessions and an individual tutorial. The classroom work was divided into an ESL component and a cross-cultural/teaching component. The course has subsequently been offered during three academic terms.

The experience of developing the course has brought with it a variety of insights concerning the needs of the foreign TAs. It is apparent that they need to concentrate on specific language problems in an intensive, individualized tutorial program. They also need practice in performing a range of teaching tasks which can be followed by group and individual feedback sessions.

The ESL component of the foreign TA course is designed to place the TA in a variety of classroom situations requiring different types of interactional skills (see Appendix A). The teaching tasks include simulating the first day of class; defining a specialized term or concept; fielding student questions; giving oral instructions; explaining a diagram, model, or illustration; presenting a short lecture; and leading a group discussion.

During the class sessions the TAs are not only expected to make their own presentations, but also to evaluate the performances of other TAs. As the course continues, the TAs assume major responsibility for providing useful feedback to the presenters. An atmosphere of trust and openness gradually emerges among the TAs in the class, helping them develop self-confidence and the ability to evaluate themselves in their own roles as teachers. Self-evaluation is encouraged throughout the course in the development of both teaching and language skills. In order to become more effective classroom teachers, however, they also learn to integrate these skills with an understanding of the cultural variables involved in classroom interaction.

## Method

In evaluating the effectiveness of the course, a case study method was adopted. This method made it possible to interpret the TAs' evaluative responses on a questionnaire concerning the course in relation to their success as classroom teachers (a copy of the questionnaire is given in Appendix B). An attempt was made to determine whether the TA had successfully integrated into the academic community and the extent to which success could be attributed to the foreign TA training course.

The evaluative questionnaire was divided into a set of introspective questions focusing on the TAs' feelings about their actual teaching experiences, and a set of retrospective questions concerning the foreign TA training course which had been completed twelve to fifteen months prior to the investigation. Both sets of questions were open-ended and were intended to allow the TAs to comment at length on their own development and on the various aspects of the course.

The following procedure was used. Ten TAs (eight men and two women) who had completed the course were given the three-page questionnaire. They were asked to give factual information, including TOEFL scores, positions held in their departments, and an estimate of their amount of daily interaction with English speakers. They were also asked to rate themselves in the areas of listening, pronunciation, speaking, composition, and grammar. The questionnaires were completed prior to individual interviews.

Using the questionnaire as a guide, two instructors of the foreign TA course conducted interviews with each of the TAs. The TAs were given an opportunity to expand on Parts II and III of the questionnaire. The interviewers were not interested in eliciting any particular kind of response, but rather in creating an atmosphere in which the TAs would feel comfortable discussing their teaching and the effectiveness of the foreign TA course. Their oral responses were used as a means of assessing their spoken English proficiency and attitudes toward teaching. Having served as foreign TA course instructors, the interviewers were in a position to comment on longitudinal changes in language proficiency and attitude. The interview information was used to complement the other sources of evaluation, such as direct observations of classroom teaching, interviews with colleagues and supervisors, and student opinion surveys.

## Results

In their evaluations of the foreign TA course, the TAs reacted to the most and least useful components of the course. There appeared to be agreement that videotaping, follow-up tutorials, peer teaching practice, and individual exercises on language difficulties were the most valuable features of the course.

Most of the TAs felt that the course helped them improve their English language skills. Some commented that they had seen no marked improvement in their language skills. However, they were at least aware of what their problems were and of what specific kinds of practice might help them improve. Most of the TAs found the teaching component of the course quite useful. They gained a new appreciation of the importance of communication with an audience and also became aware of the need to adapt, to an appropriate extent, to student expectations in the American classroom. Several of the TAs stated that the course was too short to deal effectively with the problems facing the foreign TA. Only one felt that the course was not useful.

A more detailed case-by-case analysis made it possible to complement the written data with the deeper insights that could be gained through the interview process. In considering individual cases, an interpretation of each TA's evaluative statements was made. From an analysis of these statements, it was possible to construct four distinct profiles or types grouped according to two factors: first, whether the TAs in question had decided to continue working as teachers in an American classroom after taking the TA course, as opposed to working under a professor as a research assistant (RA) or as a paper-grader; and second, whether the TAs' evaluations of themselves as speakers of English and as classroom teachers were consistent with external evaluations (interviews, classroom observations, and comments from academic advisers, supervisors and colleagues, and students). The combinations of these categories are depicted in Figure 1.

|  | *Decision re: Teaching* | |
|---|---|---|
| *Self-Evaluation* | Did not continue | Did continue |
| Consistent with external evaluation | A (n = 2) | B (n = 5) |
| Not consistent with external evaluation | C (n = 1) | D (n = 2) |

Figure 1. *Categories of foreign teaching assistants in the case-study approach to evaluating a training course.*

*Category A:* In this category are the TAs whose evaluations of themselves matched external evaluations, but who chose not to teach. This choice appeared to be based on their concern for high standards in education, which, in their view, depended greatly upon the teacher's ability to communicate effectively in English. These TAs were aware of the inadequacies in their communication skills and felt that they needed more specific training before taking on the responsibilities of teaching in the American classroom. They consistently made efforts to improve, but by the end of the course, they were still not satisfied with their improvement and chose not to teach.

The first TA in this category came to Minnesota from another university in the U.S. where he had earned an M.A. in mass communications without having to demonstrate proficiency in English. He had written his thesis and all of his papers in his native language. Upon arrival at Minnesota, he was required to take courses in English as a second language before pursuing his Ph.D. One year after fulfilling the minimum ESL requirement and having studied at the Ph.D. level, he voluntarily returned to the ESL program and expressed doubts about the adequacy of his English. He wanted to support himself with a teaching assistantship, but his lack of proficiency for teaching in the English language made him hesitant to do so. He then enrolled in the course for foreign TAs.

By viewing his videotapes with the instructor of the foreign TA course, he was able to understand how his language differed from that of native speakers of English. He began to monitor himself carefully and to improve his English. Even though he did manage to improve, he chose not to teach because of his concern for the educational needs of American students. He still felt his skills were inadequate for a regular teaching assistantship in his department, but he would lecture in English on special occasions.

Among the ten case studies there is a second example of a TA whose decision not to continue teaching was also based upon feelings of language inadequacy. As a research assistant in a clinical field, he realized that the Americans with whom he came in contact were not understanding him. During the TA course he learned how to interact more effectively with clients, but his speaking skills remained clearly inadequate for classroom teaching. However, it is interesting to note that even his academic adviser would not tell him that his pronunciation was unintelligible.

When interviewed eighteen months after completing the course, the TA reported that he had worked six months with a speech therapist but had finally given up hope of becoming a classroom TA. He reluctantly chose to support himself by working as a test-grader.

*Category B:* The five case studies that comprise the second category are those TAs who evaluated themselves in essentially the same way they were evaluated by others and who chose to continue teaching. They were aware of the factors inhibiting their successful communication with American undergraduate students, but nevertheless, chose to support themselves as classroom teachers. They developed strategies for integrating into the academic environment and for coping with their classroom communication problems. Through the TA course, they became aware of obstacles to communication and took steps to improve. They learned from the TA course that the success of their own courses also depended in part on the cooperation and motivation of the students. They recognized their own need to develop techniques for interacting with American students who had never encountered a non-native speaker of English in the role of classroom teacher.

Although each of the five TAs in this category had unique problems in the areas of language and teaching, their evaluations of themselves were consistent with external evaluations which were based on classroom observations, interviews, student evaluations, and comments from people they worked with on a daily basis. TAs in this group tended to rate their proficiency in the various skills in English as either good or fair with pronunciation consistently given the latter rating. They felt there was slight improvement in their ability to use English for teaching, but all of these TAs felt confident about teaching, and most of them had noted improvement in their teaching since they had begun working as TAs.

The most salient characteristic shared by TAs in this group was their concern that their students understand them. One TA emphasized the importance of being able to pass on her knowledge to her students. In order to succeed in this endeavor, she found it was essential to understand her American students in order to succeed in this. Her attitude was shared by the other TAs in this category. They actively sought feedback from their students regarding communication in the classroom. An analysis of their successful integration showed that each of them had a different set of needs, but that all of them had either very little or no previous teaching experience.

*Category C:* In this category is a TA who chose not to continue as a classroom teacher and whose evaluation of herself did not match the external evaluations. She lacked self-confidence, although her colleagues and supervisors believed she had excellent language skills and considerable potential for classroom teaching. Interviews with her and videotapes of her teaching led to the same conclusions. She rated her proficiency as *fair* in all skills except composition, in which she rated herself as *poor*.

As a person of small stature, this TA faced the problem of projecting her soft voice over the background noise in lab science classes. Even in traditional lecture settings, her students found it difficult to hear her. She attempted to solve this problem by using a microphone but found the situation unsatisfactory and decided to support herself as a research assistant rather than as a classroom teacher.

*Category D:* In the final category are the TAs who decided to continue as classroom teachers, yet whose evaluations of themselves did not match external evaluations. These TAs are of particular concern in contrast to those in Category B, who also continued teaching. From the sample, there are two TAs in this category.

The first is a teacher of an introductory lab course who had considerable teaching experience before coming to the United States. When asked how he felt about his teaching, he responded in writing that it was a perfect way to learn English. He felt that 90 to 95 percent of foreign TAs are effective teachers and that if their students did not understand them, the students need only to "watch and learn." He felt he had no problems in teaching or in using English despite the fact that his TOEFL score barely met the minimum requirements of his department at the time of his admission to graduate school. He rated his skills in all language areas as *good*. As for the evaluative questionnaires filled out by his students every term, he read and destroyed them routinely, so none were available for this analysis.

When he was observed in the classroom for this study, both his language was highly formal and his teaching style seemed inappropriate for the situation. During the first thirty minutes of the 45-minute class period, he lectured to the twelve undergraduates by commenting on a totally prewritten outline on the blackboard.[2] He sat on a table at the side of the room and spoke in a low monotone with his eyes fixed on the board. He asked two questions during the period, but the students were unable to answer them. Student names were not used. The TA provided the answers to his questions and said that he hoped they understood. He then urged the students not to sleep.

After this observation, it was concluded that the students must have either understood the concepts being taught before the class session had begun or they had arrived at new insights during the period without choosing to interact with the TA. A third, very real possibility, of course, was that they still had not grasped the concepts by the end of the period. In any case, the TA did not modify his lecture style even though the class was small. At this point it was suspected that the TA's concept of an effective teacher did not match the expectations of the students.

The other TA in this category taught a beginning language course. He had been teaching his native language in the U.S. for four years at the time of the study. He rated himself as good in listening, speaking, and pronunciation, and as fair in grammar and composition. When he assumed his TA position, he had difficulties associated with his lack of experience in teaching and with aural comprehension. As he gained experience, he became very confident and felt that he was an effective classroom teacher. Like the first TA, he felt that his English improved through his teaching and through contact with Americans. He felt he had no problems with his teaching.

There was, however, considerable discrepancy between this TA's evaluation of himself and others' evaluations of him. In an interview it was found that his English had in fact improved markedly. He was able to understand and respond to all of the questions with little or no difficulty and appeared to be confident in his use of English. He felt that he had reached a point at which his teaching was effective and saw no need to be interested in further improvement.

A subsequent interview with his supervisor and an analysis of his students' evaluations revealed a very different profile from the one that he had given.

His supervisor had received a number of complaints about his teaching, and in her observations of him she felt that he had considerable difficulty communicating with the students in his classroom. The written evaluations of the instructor were generally favorable except for several complaints concerning the lack of clarity in his grammatical explanations in English. His students also complained about not having an opportunity to practice the target language in class. One student wrote that the teacher and the class were "seldom on the same wave length," which made learning difficult.

An analysis of a videotape of this TA's classroom teaching confirmed the discrepancy described above. The atmosphere in his classroom was highly formal with only minimal interaction between the TA and the students. It was perhaps easier for the students to accept his shortcomings as a teacher because he was teaching a foreign language not requiring exclusive dependence on English for instruction. Because he was teaching a language course and not a course in a field like math or physics, the students may have extended some degree of cultural acceptance to him that would most likely not have been extended to his counterpart in those other fields.

## Discussion

Although each of the participants entered the foreign TA course with unique characteristics and specific needs, it was possible to isolate the variables of English language proficiency, teaching skill, and attitude for each TA. The development of the four discrete categories presented in the previous section has facilitated analysis of these variables and has led to some useful generalizations about each of the variables.

Most of the TAs felt that English was their main problem. Although some TAs showed dramatic improvement in various areas of English language proficiency, this was generally not the case. As the course continued, the TAs in Category B saw the need to compensate for their lack of fluency in the classroom setting, realizing that language improvement at their level would take place only as a gradual process. These TAs were especially open to classroom strategies designed to support their oral presentations, e.g., using the blackboard to ensure that students understand particularly troublesome vocabulary items, or asking for immediate feedback on key points in the presentation.

On the other hand, the TAs in Category D, who also chose to continue teaching, remained convinced that a mastery of English was the key to being a successful classroom teacher. TAs in this group were open to activities specifically designed to improve their English language ability. They were less interested in learning strategies to support their communication with students in the classroom.

Even though language is clearly a major variable in classroom interaction, immediate or dramatic improvement in this area was not frequently observed or expected. It is extremely important that the TAs be persuaded that there are crucial variables other than English involved in overall teaching effectiveness.

In the area of teaching skills, it was found that the TAs with limited teaching experience were very open to making changes in their teaching and that, in many cases, these changes were made quickly. On the other hand, some of the TAs who had previous teaching experience entered the foreign TA course with certain preconceived notions about teaching and learning and were not as open to change or adaptation. They came into the course with specific ideas and expectations concerning their roles as teachers at an American university and left the course with essentially the same ideas. It appeared that they had decided in advance that they had certain deficiencies, particularly in language ability, which when remedied, would make them effective classroom teachers. They resisted the idea of looking at the whole range of skills and attitudes that might affect their performance as TAs. The other TAs with teaching experience chose not to teach even after taking the foreign TA course because of their respect for high standards in education. They felt that because of their inadequacies in English, they would take non-teaching positions until they had improved sufficiently. It was apparent that some of the TAs in this category could have functioned adequately as classroom teachers.

In contrast to the variable of language proficiency, dramatic improvement was frequently observed in the area of teaching skills. It was often easier for inexperienced teachers to make changes in their teaching because they generally had not developed rigid ideas concerning the best way to teach and learn. Experienced teachers, on the other hand, were faced with the difficult task of adapting their notions of teaching and learning to the expectations of their American students. For both experienced and inexperienced foreign TAs, an appropriate attitude toward differences in educational systems seemed to be essential. The TAs who were successful in this area developed an appreciation of their students' perspectives on classroom interaction.

The cultural and attitudinal variables involved in teaching are perhaps the most difficult to isolate and analyze, but at the same time, may be the most reliable predictors of success. When foreign students come to the United States, they find themselves in a very difficult situation. They may have a strong desire to integrate completely into their new environment. For many of them, this may mean trying to become like the Americans they encounter in their daily lives. Through this desire to become a part of American culture, they may try to minimize differences and emphasize similarities.

This desire to identify with Americans may be one reason that most of the foreign TAs in this study claimed that English was the primary factor determining their success in the classroom. This perception may have been the reason that some of the TAs were closed to activities designed to improve their teaching effectiveness or to increase their awareness of cultural differences in the classroom. However, the cultural differences involved in classroom teaching, including assumptions about learning, may be the source of the greatest difficulty for the foreign TA in American classrooms. Therefore, if foreign TAs are not open to analysis and discussion of these differences, their success may be severely limited.

## Conclusions

Foreign graduate students who choose to support themselves by working as TAs in American universities are faced with difficult situations. These TAs, who are required to provide quality education to their students, may encounter serious problems in classroom communication because of their level of proficiency in the English language, their teaching skills and experience, and their attitude toward classroom education.

This chapter has discussed case studies of ten foreign TAs who had taken a special course designed to improve their classroom effectiveness. Although each TA had different language needs, different levels of teaching experience, and different attitudes toward the educational process, it was possible to create four distinct categories based on (1) how the TAs evaluated themselves and were evaluated by others, and (2) whether or not they chose to continue as classroom teachers after completing the training course for foreign TAs.

The two categories of TAs who chose not to continue as classroom teachers, Categories A and C, are not of particular interest in this study because these TAs, for a variety of reasons, have made the choice to not be involved in the education of American undergraduates. On the other hand, Categories B and D include the TAs who have continued as classroom teachers.

Those in Category B, the largest group, achieved some degree of successful integration into the American classroom. Although each of them still had specific difficulties in the areas of language and teaching skills, their open attitude toward classroom education in the United States served as a moderating variable. These TAs had a realistic perception of themselves as speakers of English and as classroom teachers, as shown by the match between their evaluations of themselves and external evaluations. They saw both classroom teaching and language skills as gradual processes requiring constant attention for improvement to take place.

In contrast, the TAs in Category D, who also continued teaching, did not show the same degree of successful integration into the American classroom. These TAs had shown improvement in their English language skills, but exhibited a rigid attitude toward classroom education. They had specific preconceived notions about the educational process, which may have been a reflection of either a cultural or a personal attitude toward education. The study found that these TAs did not have a realistic perception of themselves as speakers of English or as classroom teachers. Their attitude toward improving classroom effectiveness was that if their English skills improved, they would automatically become more effective teachers. The discrepancy found between the way these TAs perceived themselves and the way others, including American undergraduate students and immediate supervisors, perceived them suggests that this category of the four requires the most immediate attention, assuming that quality education for undergraduates is a high priority.

These case studies have shown that proficiency in the English language and adequate teaching skills are essential to the foreign TA's success in the American classroom. However, the studies also indicate that the individual TA's attitude toward the educational process in the United States is a key variable in classroom effectiveness that merits further attention and research.

# Endnotes

1. An earlier version of this chapter appeared in the MinneTESOL Journal.
2. For further discussion of blackboard techniques see the chapter by Shaw and Garate, this volume.

## Appendix A. *Classroom communication for foreign TAs*

1. *Presenting a syllabus*
   The TAs present the syllabus and essential information for the course they are teaching. The focus of this first activity is on clearly presenting the pertinent information and establishing rapport with the class. (3-5 minutes)
2. *Definition of a term*
   In this activity the TAs present a definition of a special term or concept from their fields. It is essential that the TAs adapt their material to meet the general level of the audience and that the length of the presentation be kept within the prescribed time limit. (5-7 minutes)
3. *Explaining a diagram, model, or illustration*
   The TAs choose a diagram, model, or illustration from their fields to present to the class. This activity requires the TAs to use the blackboard or some other teaching aid and at the same time to maintain adequate eye contact with the class. (5-7 minutes)
4. *Giving directions to the class*
   In this activity the TAs give the class directions for drawing something (usually a geometric design or symbol). Only oral communication can be used. The class members can ask questions to focus or clarify the TAs' directions. The TAs receive immediate feedback on their success in communicating the specified information.
5. *Fielding questions*
   Questions based on each TA's previous presentation are asked by native speakers of English. The questions are audiotaped and then played for the TAs to answer. The TAs are videotaped in front of the class as they listen to, restate, and answer the questions. The class members can ask for clarification or elaboration. This activity focuses on listening skills as well as the ability to clearly and accurately restate questions.
6. *Short lecture*
   The TAs present short lectures based on topics of general interest from their fields. This activity requires the TAs to synthesize the skills emphasized in the course and is intended to give them a clear sense of what they have accomplished during the quarter. (10 minutes)
7. *Follow-up lecture*
   In this activity the TAs can draw on the information presented in the previous lecture and can assume a certain amount of shared knowledge on the part of the class members. This gives them an opportunity to clarify problems from the previous presentation and to elaborate on a specific point. (10 minutes)

Appendix B. *University of Minnesota, classroom communication skills for international TAs, follow-up questionnaire*

*Part I*

1. Name
2. Department
3. Primary area of interest
4. When did you begin your studies at the U of M?
5. How many graduate credits do you usually take per quarter?
6. When do you plan to finish your degree?
7. What types of assistantships have you held at the U of M?
8. What classes have you taught at the U of M?
9. Are you teaching this quarter?
10. How large are the classes you teach?
11. How often do you have TA meetings?
12. Native language
13. Country
14. TOEFL score
15. Michigan Test score
16. What language do you speak at home?
17. How many hours a day do you generally speak English?
18. Please give the name of at least one person who has observed your teaching or has a good idea of your proficiency in English.

*Part II*

Please rate your own proficiency in English in the following areas:

| Grammar | Very good | Good | Fair | Poor |
|---|---|---|---|---|
| Listening Comprehension | Very good | Good | Fair | Poor |
| Speaking | Very good | Good | Fair | Poor |
| Pronunciation | Very good | Good | Fair | Poor |
| Composition | Very good | Good | Fair | Poor |

(The following questions are intended for people who have been teaching during the last year.)

1. How do you feel about teaching at the U of M?
2. Have there been any changes in your teaching since you have been at the U of M?
3. If you feel your teaching has changed, what do you think the causes of the changes are?
4. Have there been any changes in your ability to use English for teaching?
5. If you feel your proficiency in English has changed, what do you think the causes of the changes are?

*Part III*

1. Thinking back on the course "Classroom Communication for International TAs" that you took, what were the most useful parts of the course for you?
2. What specific benefits did you gain from the various parts of the course?
3. As a student or TA at the University of Minnesota, what specific problems do you still have that the course did not help you with?
4. How could the course have helped you with these problems?
5. If you were a foreign TA just beginning at the U of M, would you take this course? Why or why not?

# Two Instruments for Assessing the Oral English Proficiency of Foreign Teaching Assistants[1]

## CHARLES W. STANSFIELD
## RODNEY J. BALLARD

$S$ ince 1964, the Test of English as a Foreign Language (TOEFL) has been used to assess the English language proficiency of non-native English speakers applying to undergraduate or graduate programs at U.S. and Canadian colleges and universities. The test, which has been shown to be valid and reliable when used for its intended purpose, measures the ability to understand spoken and written English in an academic context.

Because of increased interest in a standardized measure of oral language proficiency, in 1978 the staff of Educational Testing Service initiated a research project (Clark and Swinton 1979) that culminated in the development of the Test of Spoken English (TSE). This exam is a tape recorded measure of oral English proficiency in which the examinee's responses are also tape recorded. After subsequent validation in academic settings (Clark and Swinton 1980), the TSE became an operational testing program. Now in its third year of operation, the TSE provides U.S. and Canadian universities with a means of measuring the English speaking ability of international students who are being considered for teaching assistantships or for other positions that require extensive use of spoken English. As a test of oral proficiency, the TSE is a complement to the TOEFL. It is sponsored by the TOEFL Program and is administered by Educational Testing Service (ETS).

## TSE Content

The TSE takes about twenty minutes and consists of seven sections, each involving a particular speech activity. The first section is an unscored "warm up" in which the examinee responds orally to a short series of biographical questions spoken on the test tape (name, reasons for studying English, future plans, etc.). In the second section, the examinee reads aloud a printed passage of approximately 125 words and is told that scoring will be based on pronunciation and overall clarity of speech. Time is allowed for preliminary silent reading of the passage.

In the third section, the examinee sees a series of ten partial sentences and is asked to complete each sentence orally in a way that conveys meaning and is grammatically correct. Some sample items are:

1. In order to finish the assignment . . .
2. By saving our money . . .
3. While I was waiting for the bus . . .
4. Although many people liked the movie . . .
5. Because of the cold weather . . .

The fourth and fifth sections utilize picture stimuli that "tell a continuous story." After studying the drawings briefly, the examinee is asked to tell the story that the pictures show, and to include as much detail as possible. In section five the examinee looks at a single photograph and answers a series of spoken questions about the picture's content.

Section six consists of a series of spoken questions intended to elicit free and somewhat lengthy responses from the examinee. The questions require both descriptions of common objects (e.g., describe a bicycle in as much detail as you can) and open-ended expressions of opinion on familiar issues. For instance, an examinee might be asked to discuss the best way of dealing with the world food shortage. The linguistic quality and adequacy of communication, rather than the specific knowledge revealed, are considered in scoring this section.

In the seventh and final section, the examinee sees a printed schedule, such as the following schedule for an imaginary course:

*Chemistry 200*

| | |
|---|---|
| Class lectures: | Mondays and Wednesdays |
| | Anderson Hall Room 302 |
| | 9:00 10:00 a.m. |
| Laboratory: | Fridays |
| | Johnson Hall Room 302 |
| | 3:00 5:00 p.m. |
| Final examination: | Wednesday, December 10 |
| | Anderson Hall Room 302 |
| | 9:00 10:00 a.m. |
| University holidays: | Thursday, November 23 |
| | Friday November 24 |
| | No classes |

Textbook: *An Introduction to College Chemistry*, C. Clauss and C. Whitehead, Oxford University Press: 1976

The candidate is asked to describe the schedule aloud, as though informing a group of students on the first day of class.

## Overview of TSE Operational Procedures

The TSE is given at TOEFL test centers in the U.S. and abroad. It is given on scheduled TOEFL dates so that students can take both tests on the same day and at the same location. The test is given six times per year, currently during the months of August, November, December, March, May, and June.

### Administrative Procedures

Each year the exact test administration dates are published in the TSE "Examinee Application Form and Procedures." Copies of the form are distributed to all TOEFL test centers, to American embassies, binational centers, and language institutes, and to numerous other agencies and individuals interested in the TSE.[2] Often departments that require TSE scores of applicants include copies of the application form in the materials sent in response to inquiries from non-native English speaking persons. The TSE is given at TOEFL test centers throughout the world under strictly controlled testing procedures. Once a completed appplication form is received, the examinee is assigned to a test center for the date selected and sent a registration form, the TSE *Examinee Handbook*, and a disc. The *Handbook* and disc include a description of each section of the test, the test directions, and practice questions. The registration form requests information necessary to identify the examinee and the names of institutional score recipients.

### Scoring Procedures

The examinee's tapes is sent directly to ETS for scoring. TSE answer tapes are rated by official TSE raters, who are experienced teachers and specialists in the field of English as a second language. Raters are trained at one-day workshops conducted by ETS staff members.

Currently, every TSE tape is rated independently by two raters; neither person rating an individual tape knows the scores assigned by the other, and the examinee's score is the average of their two ratings. Scores are assigned on four separate criteria (overall comprehensibility, pronunciation, grammar, and fluency). If the two raters do not agree on any of the four scores, a third person listens to the answer tape and rates the areas of disagreement. In such a case, the reported scores are based on the average of the three ratings.

The overall comprehensibility criterion is designed to be a global rating of the examinee's proficiency in dealing with a variety of complex speech tasks. Overall comprehensibility scores are reported on a scale that ranges from 0 to 300; all scores are rounded to the nearest tenth. Descriptions of the performance indicated by each score range follow.

Overall Comprehensibility

0-90 Overall comprehensibility too low in even the simplest type of speech.

100-140 Generally not comprehensible due to frequent pauses and/or rephrasing, pronunciation errors, limited grasp of vocabulary, and lack of grammatical control.

150-190 Generally comprehensible but with frequent errors in pronunciation, grammar, choice of vocabulary items, and with some pauses or rephrasing.

200-240 Generally comprehensible with some errors in pronunciation, grammar, choice of vocabulary items, or with pauses or occasional rephrasing.

250-300 Completely comprehensible in normal speech, with occasional grammatical or pronunciation errors in very colloquial phrases.

## Reporting Procedures

The score reports issued for the TSE consist of an Examinee's Score Confirmation Record, which is sent to the examinee, and an official score report that is sent directly by Educational Testing Service to two institutions specified by the examinee. The official score report includes the examinee's name, native country and language, date of birth, the test date, and four different test scores: a score for overall comprehensibility and scores for the three diagnostic areas of pronunciation, grammar, and fluency. It also provides descriptions of general speech characteristics by score level for each of these criteria.

## Speaking Proficiency English Assessment Kit (SPEAK)

The TSE program also offers the Speaking Proficiency English Assessment Kit (SPEAK), which enables institutions to utilize a retired test form from the TSE international program for local placement purposes. While the TSE is designed for use in the selection and placement of graduate foreign applicants, SPEAK can be used to test those currently employed as teaching assistants or in another capacity. Using both the TSE and SPEAK, it is possible to assess the oral English proficiency of a non-native group at the time of application and at one or more points subsequent to their arrival on campus. Alternatively, one could compare overseas candidates' TSE scores with the SPEAK scores of currently employed non-native speaking TAs.

SPEAK contains all the materials needed to set up and administer a local testing program. The kit includes a self-instructional rater training manual that explains how to administer the test, how to use the overall comprehensibility and diagnostic scales to assign ratings, and how to determine the overall comprehensibility and diagnostic scores. Also included is a set of rater training tapes containing examples of actual examinee performance and an explanation of the rating assigned to each response. A set of rater testing tapes permits the rater to score a series of complete tests and to compare the scores with the actual scores assigned by language testing specialists at ETS. The kit also includes 30 reusable test booklets for examinees, one cassette and one reel-to-reel test tape for actual administration of the test, and a package of rating sheets to be used for the assignment of ratings and the calculation of scores.

SPEAK is available for direct purchase by university-affiliated English language institutes, institutional testing offices, private language schools, and other education-related organizations serving public or private educational programs. For additional information, write to SPEAK, Box 2882, Princeton, NJ 08541.

## Current Use of TSE and SPEAK

As of August 1983, TSE and SPEAK were being used by several colleges and universities (see Appendix A) to assess the spoken English skills of foreign teaching assistants and other foreign students. The state legislature of Florida recently mandated non-native speaking instructors "be proficient in the oral use of English, as determined by the Test of Spoken English . . . or a similar test" (Chronicle of Higher Education, July 7, 1983, 2). Both TSE and SPEAK are currently being considered at many other institutions in the U.S. and Canada, particularly those with large graduate programs and those admitting a large number of foreign graduate students. Institutions set their own criterion levels on these tests; typically, the standards of acceptable oral proficiency for non-native speaking TAs fall within a range of 200-250 on the overall comprehensibility scale.

The TSE is also used within the health-related professions. Currently, foreign trained veterinarians are required to submit TSE scores to the Education Commission on Foreign Veterinary Graduates, an affiliate of the American Veterinary Medicine Association. These candidates must demonstrate proficiency in spoken English as part of the process of becoming licensed to practice veterinary medicine in the United States. The TSE is also required of foreign-trained nurses applying for licensing to the Colorado State Board of Nursing. A recent research study (Powers and Stansfield 1983) shows the TSE can also be a valid measure of oral language proficiency for use in the certification or licensing of non-native English-speaking professionals in the health-related fields of medicine, nursing, pharmacy and veterinary medicine. SPEAK is also used for on-site testing by a number of government agencies and private corporations.

## Research on the TSE

As noted above, the TSE and SPEAK are commercially available tests of oral English proficiency which have been used in many situations. With the increased utilization of the TSE and SPEAK, it has been possible to conduct studies of their reliability and validity.

### Reliability of the TSE

Reliability is the extent to which a test yields consistent results. Several different types of reliability may be relevant to a single test. In the case of a test of oral language where scores are assigned by more than one rater, interrater reliability is of particular concern. When an examinee's score is based on the average of two ratings, as is currently the case, unless scores are abnormally discrepant, the interrater reliability of the two overall comprehensibility scores is .88. That is, if tests already scored by two raters were rescored by two different raters, the correlation between the two averages would be .88.[3]

As noted above, three raters are used whenever there is a substantial discrepancy between the ratings assigned by the first two raters to the overall score or any of the diagnostic subscores. Current experience indicates that a third rater is utilized about 6 percent of the time. In such cases, an estimate of the interrater reliability of the overall comprehensibility score is .92. That is, if tests scored by three raters were rescored by three different raters, the correlation between the two score averages would be .92. Because most TSE scores are based on the average of two ratings, the coefficient of .88 can be considered a fair, if not a slightly conservative, estimate of the true interrater reliability of TSE scores.

### Validity of the TSE

Validity refers to the extent to which a test actually measures what it purports to measure. If an oral language proficiency test yields very consistent scores, it can be considered reliable. However, if those scores show little relationship to real-life performance, the validity of the test is questionable. While many procedures exist for determining validity, there is no single indicator or standard index of validity. Rather, validity is established by compiling information on the nature of the test and its ability to predict certain criterion behaviors.

For nearly three decades the most widely respected test of spoken language proficiency has been the oral proficiency interview administered by the Foreign Service Institute (FSI) of the United States Department of State (Wilds 1975; Sollenberger 1978). It consists of a structured conversation of about fifteen to twenty-five minutes between the examinee and a trained interviewer who is either a native or a near-native speaker of the test language. Performance on the interview is evaluated on a scale ranging from zero to five, with level zero representing no functional ability in the language, and level five representing proficiency indistinguishable from that of an educated native speaker.

In order to determine the relationship between scores on the FSI Oral Interview and scores on the Test of Spoken English, both tests were administered to sixty foreign teaching assistants (TAs) at several large state universities (Clark and Swinton 1980). In addition, recent TOEFL scores for thirty-one of those TAs were obtained from student records. Table 1 depicts the correlations between the TSE and the other two instruments.

Table 1. *Relationship of TSE to FSI ratings and TOEFL scores\**

| TSE scale | Correlation with FSI rating | Correlation with TOEFL total score |
|---|---|---|
| Pronunciation | .77 | .56 |
| Grammar | .73 | .70 |
| Fluency | .76 | .60 |
| Comprehensibility | .76* | .57 |

*All correlation coefficients are significant at or beyond the .001 level; $n = 31$.

As can be seen, the TSE shows fairly strong correlations with FSI interview ratings, while TSE subscores other than grammar show only moderate correlations with TOEFL scores. In addition, the correlation between TSE comprehensibility and FSI ratings for all sixty TAs in the Clark and Swinton study (1980) was .79. If one accepts the FSI Oral Interview as a valid criterion measure, Clark and Swinton's findings indicate that the TSE represents a substantial improvement over TOEFL in the prediction of oral language proficiency.

Within the context of college and university instruction, the TSE was validated in the same study involving 134 foreign teaching assistants at nine universities (Clark and Swinton 1980). Here it was found that an instructor's TSE comprehensibility score correlated with students' assessment of the instructor's ability to handle common situations involving language skills. Some of these situations and their corresponding correlations were lectures ($r = .60$), understanding student questions ($r = .52$), answering questions ($r = .53$), and communication during office appointments ($r = .54$). The TSE score also correlated with the degree to which the instructor's pronunciation interfered with student understanding ($r = .68$). To a lesser extent, the TSE score predicted students' evaluations of the instructor's overall teaching performance ($r = .29$, $n = 34$, $p < .01$).

In addition to language skills, overall performance or teaching effectiveness is determined by several other factors, such as organization, class preparation, interpersonal relations, accessibility, originality, assigned workload, and evaluation procedures. The fact that the TSE comprehensibility score correlates with teaching effectiveness may also indicate that degree of English language proficiency influences or otherwise correlates with these factors. In the Clark and Swinton study, the TSE score did not correlate significantly with student ratings of the instructor's knowledge of the subject.

## Concluding Remarks

One way in which the TSE or SPEAK can be used is in helping academic departments to establish criterion levels of acceptable comprehensibility among foreign teaching assistants. The TSE program has developed a sample tape that contains examinee responses to selected TSE passages at ten different score levels, arranged in order from low score to high score. The tape may be used by departmental or institututional committees responsible for establishing initial score requirements. Such committees could include both faculty and student representatives.

Once an initial standard is set, departments or institutions should conduct follow-up studies on the validity of the score standard. This research may be conducted by the local office of institutional research, by the university testing service, or by a graduate student in education or psychology in fulfillment of a thesis requirement. A correlation coefficient between student ratings and TSE scores can be useful in establishing local validity. Expectancy tables can be used to show the distribution of levels of teaching performance, as rated by students, for instructors with given English proficiency scores. The expectancy tables can be portrayed by department, and can be considered in subsequent discussions to raise or lower the standard. Additional information on local validation of standards is available in the *TSE Manual for Score Users*, in Powers and Stansfield (1983), and in Livingston and Zieky (1982). Further information about the TSE and SPEAK, including the *TSE Manual for Score Users* and a sample tape, can be obtained by contacting the TSE Director, Department T10, Educational Testing Service, Princeton, NJ 08541.[4]

## Endnotes

1. An earlier version of this chapter was presented at the 1983 NAFSA Annual Conference in Cincinnati by Charles W. Stansfield.
2. A supply of these forms can be obtained from TSE, Box 2882, Princeton, NJ, 08541.
3. Further information about the test's reliability is found in the *TSE Manual for Score Users*.
4. The TSE program office attempts to monitor the use of TSE by agencies and institutions that utilize the test service. Thus, institutions conducting local validation studies are requested to forward a copy of the findings to the TOEFL Program Research Coordinator.

Appendix A.  *Users of TSE and SPEAK as of August 1983*

| Institutions with one or more departments requiring or requesting TSE scores | Institutions using SPEAK |
| --- | --- |
| University of Florida | University of Alabama |
| University of California at Los Angeles | University of Texas at San Antonio |
| Oklahoma State University | Newport College |
| University of Illinois | University of Georgia |
| University of Arizona | Ohio University |
| University of Wisconsin | State University of New York at Buffalo |
| Northwestern University | American University |
| University of Delaware | University of Dallas |
| University of Maryland | University of California at Santa Cruz |
| University of Missouri | Pennsylvania State University |
| University of Central Florida | University of South Carolina |
| University of Arkansas | Indiana State University |
| Iowa State University | University of Tennessee |
| Monterey Institute of International Studies | State University of New York at Stony Brook |
| | North Texas State University |
| | Creighton University |
| | University of Manitoba, Winnipeg, Canada |
| | University of Guelph, Guelph, Canada |
| | Nazan University, Nogoya, Japan |
| | World Economic Information Services, Tokyo |
| | Naval Postgraduate School, Monterey, CA |
| | Pomona Valley Community Hospital, Pomona, CA |
| | Columbia College, Vancouver, Canada |
| | Queens College, NY |
| | Thai International Airways |
| | Syracuse University |
| | University of Maryland |

# A Typology of Teaching Assistants[1]

## Kathleen M. Bailey

Our awareness of "the foreign TA problem" is largely a result of students' complaints about non-native speakers employed as TAs in U.S. universities. Unfortunately, though not surprisingly, these complaints tend to be rather vague. "He can't speak English" and "You can't understand a word he says" are not particularly useful comments in any diagnostic sense.

In order to better understand what exactly students were complaining about, I arranged to visit the classes of non-native speakers working as TAs at UCLA. The departments of math and physics were chosen for the on-site observations because these two departments had the most letters of complaint on record regarding non-native speaking TAs. In addition, courses in these two departments afforded a combination of both discussion sections and laboratory settings.

Six pairs of TAs were chosen in each department from among a pool of forty-four TAs who were willing to be observed. Each pair consisted of a non-native speaking Asian TA matched with a native speaker teaching in a different section of the same course during the same quarter. Non-native speaking TAs were paired with native speakers in this study so that, by comparison, I could detect both "errors of omission" and "errors of commission." It is possible that some of the students' complaints were based on what the foreign TAs failed to do as well as what they did. Asian TAs were chosen because in a pilot study they had been identified as the group having the most difficulty adjusting to the educational system at UCLA. The twelve foreign TAs in the observational sample were native speakers of Chinese, Korean, and Japanese. All these TAs were males.

All of the classes observed were regularly scheduled lower-division undergraduate courses. In each department three of the courses were designed for majors in that discipline and the other three were designed for non-majors.

Students' evaluations of these twenty-four TAs were made available to me at the end of the quarter. A comparison of the scores showed that the students rated the native speakers significantly higher than the foreign TAs. However, there were no significant differences between the ratings of the math TAs as a group and those of the physics TAs, nor was there any interaction effect.

The classes were visited during the beginning, middle, and end of the academic quarter. During each observation I took extensive fieldnotes, documenting the TA's speech, his patterns of movement through the classroom, his nonverbal behavior, and evidence of his relationship with the students. After each observation the rough notes were recopied and details were added. The data upon which the following typology is based consisted of 1,197 pages of finalized fieldnotes. In the fieldnotes, the 24 TAs were identified by pseudonyms, some of which are also used in the following discussion.

## TA Typology

The fieldnotes for each observation were summarized, and then the summaries of each TA's performance were synthesized to form a profile that characterized the subject's behavior over the ten-week quarter. The profiles of the twenty-four teaching assistants were then compared to identify possible models or types of TAs. Five types emerged in this analysis. Each type was given a descriptive label and one TA profile was selected to represent the type. The typological names are intended to capture a generalization about the behaviors of the group members. (For a more complete discussion of the research methodology and sampling issues involved in this study, see Bailey 1982a).

### Type 1: Active Unintelligible TAs

The first type of TA can be characterized as physically active, fast-talking, knowledgeable, but unintelligible. There were three foreign TAs in this group, two Koreans and a native speaker of Chinese. All three were able to do the students' homework. They could all talk and write at the same time, providing explication as they solved the problems at the blackboard. They were also physically active and appeared confident. They used a variety of hand and arm gestures, although these gestures were not always clearly synchronized with the meaning of their English utterances.

These three TAs shared linguistic characteristics as well. Their speech was so heavily accented that they were difficult for the students to understand. They tended to talk very quickly, which often compounded their pronunciation problems. Although they apparently understood students' questions and comments with little difficulty, the students were not always able to understand these TAs. Syntactic errors were common in their speech, especially in the cases of the two Koreans, who produced noticeable subjectless or verbless sentences.

These TAs often asked questions or encouraged the students to speak, but many such utterances were simply follow-ups to initial misunderstandings. They frequently encouraged students to come to their office hours and announced additional help sessions before exams. Yet their efforts apparently went unappreciated since they were rated very low in the student evaluations. The following profile of Park illustrates the classroom communication problems of an Active Unintelligible TA.

## Profile of Park

Park is a native speaker of Korean who led a physics discussion section for students majoring in physics, math, or engineering. The section met in a large lecture hall with an amphitheater floor plan.

Park was apparently competent in his discipline, and tried very hard to explain the material to the students, but his spoken English presented serious problems. His speech could be characterized as fast but inaccurate. Park's grammar and accent were especially faulty. There were numerous errors in basic sentence structure, including subjectless and verbless sentences and morphology problems (e.g., using a noun as a verb or vice versa). These "basic" syntactic problems are puzzling since they were sometimes juxtaposed with well-formed complex sentences.[2]

Park's difficulties with the pronunciation of English consonants were typical of many Korean adults learning English. (For example, "s" is sometimes pronounced like "sh," "l" like "r" and vice versa, and word-initial "w" may seem to disappear.) But the main source of Park's difficulty was the suprasegmental patterns of English. He sometimes broke his phrases at non-phrase boundaries, inserting pauses at unexpected points. He also overused rising intonation within sentences, perhaps to check the students' understanding of the material, his English, or both. This combination of inappropriate phrase boundaries and the list-like rising intonation gave Park's speech a looping, repetitive, sing-song quality. (Park realized that his pronunciation was problematic. He had even voluntarily taken a course to improve his accent.)

These phonological and grammatical problems were compounded by the speed with which Park spoke. He talked as fast as any of the native speaking TAs, and even faster than some. Although there were occasional false starts in his speech, Park seemed to be a confident speaker of English. He also answered students' questions without hesitation. However, the pace of his speech, coupled with his accent and the numerous grammar errors, sometimes made it impossible to understand him.

The speed at which Park spoke gave his discussion section a rushed quality, which was exacerbated by his nonverbal behavior. At each of the three observations he hurried into the lecture hall (sometimes late), talked and wrote quickly, moved fast, only partially erased the blackboard, and generally rushed through the problems. Items he dropped (the chalk, an eraser) were left on the floor or kicked aside. Once after an observation I told Park I hoped I had not made him nervous. He responded with, "No, no! No time to nervous!" (sic).

Part of the impression of haste he created was due to Park's physical movements, but his nonverbal behaviors sometimes aided his efforts to communicate. His motions were purposeful and fluid, so he looked confident and physically balanced. He was very mobile and used much of the blackboard space in the amphitheater, but he shuffled his feet as he walked back and forth beside the blackboard. He gestured boldly with his hands and arms as he spoke. Usually these gestures helped convey the meaning, but at other times they seemed random. Occasionally he talked toward the blackboard as he wrote and then failed to re-establish eye contact with the students when he had finished. He sometimes asked a question without looking at the students and then answered it himself when no one volunteered a response.

These problems in Park's communication skills were apparent in all three observations. Yet it was also obvious that he was trying very hard to help the students. He attempted to answer all their questions and seemed prepared for class. Before the midterm exam he invited the students to come to his office for additional help (even on a Saturday). The offer for an extra study session was made again before the final exam. During the last class session he twice encouraged the students to come to his office hours. He also gave them some tips about solving equations and about what to expect on the exam.

But, as might be expected, the students did not seem to respond to Park's efforts. Many appeared restless during the class. Some asked questions that seemed to challenge Park's knowledge and/or authority. Some talked together privately as Park tried to conduct the session. I heard sighs, exasperated exhalations, and snickering or snorting sounds from the students. There was laughter among a group of male students after one of them belched loudly. Others came in late and left early. Some changed seats during the discussion section in order to sit near friends and chat. In general, the group conveyed an attitude of annoyance with the TA. The students seemed to tolerate Park rather than to cooperate with him.

## Type 2: Mechanical Problem Solvers

The second TA category in the observational sample includes one native speaker and five non-native speakers of English. These six teachers were all competent in their subject matter. That is, they were able to solve and explain the students' homework problems and conduct physics labs. Thus, like the active unintelligible TAs, they are characterized as knowledgeable.

However, the mechanical problem solvers differ from the former group in that they seemed relatively passive and quiet. In fact, they spoke so quietly that it was sometimes difficult to hear them over the general noise in the environment. In addition, there were often periods of silence in the classrooms of these TAs as they wrote on the blackboard or silently watched the students conduct the experiments. Although they were able to write and talk simultaneously, they did so less regularly than other TAs in the sample. When they did talk, their speech was relatively slow and deliberate.

Physically, these TAs were also somewhat passive in the classroom. Compared to other TAs in the sample, they seldom used hand or arm movements to underscore the meaning of their utterances. Their eye contact with students was also less frequent and of shorter duration than that of the other TAs.

In terms of classroom discourse patterns, the mechanical problem solvers elicited less input from the students than their peers. They also shared less personal information and offered little encouragement to their students. Although there is some variation in their behavior, as a group these TAs tended to react to the students, rather than directing the classroom interaction.

## Profile of Kwan

Kwan was a native speaker of Chinese who was the TA for a math discussion section. There were seldom many students in his section and those who did come tended to trickle in late and leave early. At the first meeting there were eighteen students present. During two other observations there were only three students one day and seven on another—which happened to be the day before an exam. At one of my scheduled observations, no students appeared at all. These low attendance patterns may be related to Kwan's teaching style.

At the first class meeting Kwan wrote his name, office hours, office number, and the course number on the board, but he told the students nothing about his background and asked nothing about them (e.g., he apparently did not try to learn their names). There were no "getting-to-know-you" remarks—no comments about the course or himself to put the students at ease. In short, Kwan made no effort to build rapport with the students.[3]

Kwan's classroom style was rather passive. Much of this impression was based on nonlinguistic signals. He seldom used gestures to support the meaning of his speech. When he was not writing, his arms hung limply by his sides—and even when he was writing, his other hand was inactive. His voice was soft, and he sometimes mumbled or talked toward the blackboard. There was little or no difference between the volume or pitch he used as he spoke to the students and that he used as he did calculations on the blackboard. He did not project his voice when addressing the class; it was as if he were talking to himself. There were also periods of silence as the TA wrote on the board, read his math book, or awaited the students' questions.

Kwan didn't call on students during any of the classroom observations. Instead he would stand silently, waiting for them to ask questions. Then he would usually work problems (rather than explaining them) in response to their requests. In fact, writing seemed to be his main channel for communicating with the students. Indeed, he had what could be called "good blackboard technique" (i.e., clear handwriting, organized lay-out of solutions on the board, boxes drawn around the answers, vertical lines drawn to separate completed portions of problems from new work, etc.). But as a result of Kwan's involvement with the blackboard, there was relatively little eye contact between him and the students. Instead he would look at the problem and occasionally glance back at the students, with the blackboard holding his attention.

One result of Kwan's seeming passivity, distance, and lack of exuberance was that the students ran the class most of the time. They were in control of the discourse and Kwan reacted to them. In each observation the students talked to one another about the math, with a great deal of on-task, overt peer-teaching, as if they were being TAs for each other, explaining further or expanding on what Kwan had said. In fact, Kwan did not seem to explain much. He was like a problem-solving machine: he worked the problems and the students watched. They would ask him questions, but much of the elaboration and explanation was generated by the students instead of the TA. To be sure, there was some give-and-take, but Kwan could not be characterized as having an interactive teaching style. As a result, the students set the pace and kept the lessons going—in effect cooperating with one another to digest the TA's demonstration solutions. Yet there were possible symptoms of boredom among the students (yawning, stretching, early departure, developing side conversations).

Ironically, Kwan's English was not a serious problem. Although there was occasional switching of "l" and "r," his pronunciation was quite intelligible. His grammar errors did not seem to interfere with the students' ability to understand him. He spoke at a slow steady pace, suggesting neither great fluency nor a lack of fluency. Although he occasionally repeated words or phrases verbatim, possibly indicating a restricted vocabulary, Kwan apparently understood the students' questions and responded to them without hesitation. In sum, even though his spoken English was not native-like, it was not really problematic; but his passivity and inappropriate paralinguistic behavior made him seem inept.

Thus Kwan's major classroom communication problems can be attributed to the fact that he either did not understand the role of the TA or he was unwilling (or unable) to assume it. Noticeably, he never approximated the role of a TA as a knowledgeable helpmate and friend. There were no smiles, jokes, laughter, or off-task comments, no sharing of personal information in any of his observations.

## Type 3: Knowledgeable Helpers/Casual Friends

The third category, the largest group of TAs in the observational sample, consisted of six native speakers and two non-native speakers. Like the active unintelligible TAs and the mechanical problem solvers, all the members of this group were competent in their disciplines. They could all solve the students' homework problems or conduct physics labs. In addition, the members of this group clearly demonstrated purposeful teaching behaviors. Efforts to explain, to clarify, to paraphrase, and to demonstrate were typical of their classroom discourse. They were helpful and generally friendly to the students, and there were occasional flashes of on-task humor. However, the tone of their classes was business-like, with the TA either in control or quickly able to regain control.

The members of this group also differed from the previous types in that they could be easily heard and understood. This is not surprising, since three-fourths of the group were native speakers of English. However, this was also true of the two foreign TAs in this group.

Both of these non-native speakers seemed to enact the role of a TA as knowledgeable helper and casual friend to the students (as did the native speakers in the group). In the fieldnotes, there were no records of complaints from the students or observed negative behavior toward either of these TAs.

## Profile of Lim

Lim is a native speaker of Chinese who led a physics lab section for life science majors. He had a very interactive teaching style. In all three observations, he elicited information from the students during the explanation of the experiment. He waited patiently after posing questions and then restated his questions if the students did not respond. He often confirmed their ideas by saying "Yes" and repeating or paraphrasing their answers to his questions. In each observation he checked to see what material had been covered in the professor's lectures. He also consistently gave the students helpful hints about conducting the experiments and tips on how to write the lab reports correctly.

In terms of his nonverbal behavior, Lim appeared confident, animated, and relaxed. He used hand and arm gestures which supported the meaning of his utterances. He maintained regular eye contact with the class as he talked. In addition, he was able to use the blackboard to advantage, consistently drawing diagrams and pointing to them during his explanations of the labs. He often smiled and the students laughed at his pleasantries. He seemed to think of the students as near-equals: they called him by his first name and he sometimes used the inclusive forms we and let's.

Lim's control of English, while clearly not "native," was usually sufficient.[4] Each set of fieldnotes includes an observation that the TA spoke loudly and clearly, indicating his understanding of the appropriate paralinguistic features of teaching discourse. Although his speech was accented and occasionally sounded somewhat choppy, Lim was usually easy to understand. There are three instances recorded in the fieldnotes of my having misunderstood a word, but in each case the TA was able to make himself understood. For example, during one class, Lim told the students, "If you prove this, you get some bonus mark," but the last two words were unclear. He immediately wrote bonus mark on the blackboard, perhaps in response to a non-verbal cue from a student which I did not see. Although a native speaker of American English might have said "extra credit" instead, Lim quickly clarified his comment by resorting to the written mode.

Lim's speech revealed occasional grammar errors, including missing third person singular -s, lacking the plural -s in places, and no inversion of the subject and auxiliary verb in some questions. However, errors of these sorts were more sporadic than regular. Once he admitted in class that he was often confused as to whether a word was *permeativity* or *permeability,* but then he used the latter form correctly in his explanation.

More significant than his occasional grammar errors was Lim's versatility in the different uses of speech associated with teaching discourse. Lim's verbal repertoire included greetings at the beginning of the lab sessions, occasional jokes, confirmations, hints, tips, elicitations, and apologies when students pointed out errors on the blackboard. He also provided reassurances, as when he told the students, following a complicated point, "Don't worry about it. I will put this on the blackboard later."

In addition, Lim's explanations were well structured. For instance, at one point in a lengthy explanation, he reminded the students of what they would have already done in the first part of the lab by the time they got to the section he was describing. In this way, he seemed to knit the lesson together and provide a better overall picture of the experiment for the students.

All the TAs categorized as knowledgeable helpers/casual friends demonstrated purposeful teaching behaviors. This characteristic is illustrated in the length of Lim's explanations. In each of the three observations, Lim used the first forty-five to fifty minutes of a two-hour lab period to explain the experimental procedures and the theory behind them. This was longer than the time taken for explanations by the other lab TAs in the observational sample. However, Lim's students never exhibited symptoms of boredom or restlessness, as did the students in the classes of the mechanical problem solvers. Instead, they responded to his questions, asked questions of their own, and murmured answers as he talked, seemingly involved in and following his explanations.

Lim was apparently successful as a TA, while other non-native speakers with similar language proficiency were not. Some factors contributing to his success may have been his sense of humor, his apparent confidence, the fact that he was helpful to the students, his organized presentations and clear drawings, and the relatively interactive teaching style he used.

## Type 4: Entertaining Allies

This group consisted of two native speakers of English: Mark, a physics lab TA, and Dan, a math TA. Both taught courses for non-majors. Like the other types of TAs, both Dan and Mark were competent in their subject matter. Dan solved and explained the students' math homework problems, while Mark conducted and supervised the physics experiments with apparent ease. These two TAs differed from the previously discussed TA types, however, in their consistent use of humor in the classroom.

Mark's use of humor in the physics lab was very interactive. He seemed to encourage light banter between himself and the students, although he usually restricted the playfulness to the task at hand. During one lab session as the students did the experiment Mark asked, "Okay, who's got problems?" A male student responded, "I've got all kinds of problems. You wanna hear about them?" Mark told him to write to Dear Abby. When another student made a mistake in an experiment Mark said, "No, no, no! Well, I'm afraid your academic career is over. I'll visit you at Venice Beach while you're there swilling Ripple." Some students laughed and asked him if he had seen them at that beach, since they went there often.

In addition to entertaining the students and explaining the subject matter clearly, Dan and Mark also gave signals that they were the students' allies. They both overtly thanked students for information, praised the students' questions and correct answers, encouraged them to ask further questions, and often gave them tips about solving problems, doing the labs, and taking exams.

These TAs' linguistic characteristics also emphasized the ways in which Dan and Mark were like their students. Both of them adopted a casual, conversational style of classroom discourse, which included frequent use of phonologically reduced forms, such as *gonna, wanna, hafta, gotta,* etc. They both regularly used the inclusive pronouns *we, our,* and *us.* Thus in their respective classrooms, Dan and Mark seemed to take positions as knowledgeable group members rather than as distant authority figures. When a student asked Dan about mandatory attendance at the discussion section, the TA said, "I don't take roll."

These two TAs also seemed to have a sense of their students as an audience. Both constantly used hand and arm gestures that underscored the meaning of their utterances. Both looked back over their shoulders at the students as they wrote on the blackboard, typically maintaining (rather than re-establishing) eye contact with the students. These TAs were both physically mobile and smiled, or even grinned, much of the time. They both seemed to enjoy their subjects, their teaching, and their students. The students responded by attending their classes regularly, staying actively involved in the lessons, and giving them high marks on their teaching evaluations.

## Profile of Dan

Dan is a native speaker of English who taught a low-level math class for life science majors. In addition to apparently knowing the subject matter, Dan explained it with confidence and enthusiasm. His discussion sections were enlivened by his consistent use of humor, including puns, word play, and humorous anecdotes. For example, when he said, "Do *U*" in explaining the steps of a problem, he then played with the meanings of "do you" and "do ewe."

However, this light-hearted tone did not mean Dan was wasting time. On the contrary, his humor was "on-task." He used it in the process of explaining, to help students understand the math concepts he covered. He also incorporated shared cultural knowledge into his humorous explanations of mathematical concepts. For instance, Dan explained *average velocity* through an extended impromptu narrative about a hypothetical driving trip from Los Angeles to San Francisco, which included stopping at Pea Soup Andersen's (a restaurant about midway between), getting a speeding ticket, and shooting at a highway patrolman. The students laughed as Dan made up the story. While he talked he drew a line graph on the blackboard which depicted the relationship between distance and speed on his make-believe journey. The students laughed again as Dan said, "This is a bad graph. This actually has me going in reverse here. . . ." Such humor was typical of his explanations. During Dan's class the students often laughed and they appeared to enjoy his lessons.

Dan also used a variety of teaching strategies to his advantage. These included restatements and paraphrases, rhetorical questions to structure the discourse, and overt definitions (i.e., those preceded by some sort of verbal announcement of a definition to follow, such as "By 'distinguished' I mean . . ."). He also gave the students real-world examples (e.g., talking about smog in illustrating linearity) and hints which allowed *them* to solve the problems they had asked him about. He tried to make math both clear and fun.

Dan's nonverbal and paralinguistic behavior facilitated communication. He used a casual speech style, talking quickly, loudly, and clearly. He gestured almost constantly, using hand and arm movements that emphasized the meaning of his verbal explanations. His facial expressions were lively too. He often smiled broadly and winked at the students when he made a joke or when they indicated sudden understanding of a concept. He would frequently look back over his shoulder at the class as he wrote on the blackboard. Sometimes he stepped away from the board and looked at it from the students' vantage point. Physically he exuded enthusiasm almost to the point of nervous energy.

Dan seemed very happy about his role as the students' ally. He often encouraged them to ask questions. He reponded with "Sure!" when a student asked if he would work another problem for her. At the first class meeting he arranged his office hours after polling the students about a convenient time for them (but joked that it had to be before three in the afternoon because after that he would be at the race track). He also told the students that while doing word problems, "you just gotta try to stay sane." Dan's encouragement seemed to provide the students with affective support while they struggled with the math concepts he taught.

## Type 5: The Inspiring Cheerleaders

The two TAs in this category were Alan, a physics discussion leader, and Lan, a math TA. Alan, a native speaker of English, appears to be the students' ideal teaching assistant, since he was rated highest in the student evaluations of these teachers. Lan, a native speaker of Chinese, was ranked third out of the twenty-four TAs on overall teaching effectiveness.

Alan and Lan both taught at eight o'clock in the morning, which may suggest that they and their students were energetic early risers. Alan's students were physics, math, and engineering majors who met with him once a week in a large lecture hall for the discussion section supplementing a professor's lectures, while Lan's were non-majors enrolled in his remedial math class. It met every day and he was the sole teacher for the course. In spite of the apparent differences between the two groups of students, Alan and Lan used some remarkably similar teaching behaviors.

One of the most notable characteristics of the two inspiring cheerleaders was the high level of positive affect in their classrooms. Both TAs learned and consistently used their students' first names in class, which was strikingly different from the behavior of all the other TAs in the observational sample. In calling their students by name, these TAs seemed to recognize them as individuals. Such acknowledgement may be a rare experience for freshmen enrolled in large lecture classes. The students were on a first-name basis with Alan and Lan as well.

Alan and Lan were also friendly and supportive toward their students. Their use of the inclusive pronouns we, our, and us was noticeable. They praised, encouraged, cajoled, and generally seemed to value their students as individuals. They communicated an almost cheerleader-like enthusiasm for the subject matter. Their attitudes toward the students and the work seemed to be, "We're in this together and it's great fun!"

However, Alan and Lan's success was not based only on their rapport with the students. Both were skillful teachers who took their roles seriously. In each observation they both worked from prepared lesson plans. Their explanations, which were easily understood, were usually communicated in all three channels available to a teacher: the oral, the graphic, and the gestural modes. They could easily be heard at the back of the room, and their blackboard drawing and writing were clear and legible. In working with concepts, Alan and Lan both dealt with the homework problems incrementally, making sure the students understood what had been done before proceeding.

All of these teaching characteristics taken together meant that the students did not have to struggle to understand either Alan or Lan. They could concentrate instead on mastering the subject matter.

These two TAs seemed to inspire the students with enthusiasm for math and physics. Part of this impression of enthusiasm is based on the TAs' nonverbal behavior. Both Alan and Lan were physically active in the classroom, moving confidently through the teacher's zone, using hand and arm gestures and whole body motions to underscore the meaning of their words. They maintained regular eye contact with the students, including those in the most distant corners of the rooms. They often smiled and their facial expressions frequently revealed happiness, even joy, as they taught. Unlike Dan and Mark, the entertaining allies, who typically communicated humor, Lan and Alan (whose classes were by no means devoid of humor) consistently projected infectious, almost boyish enthusiasm and high positive expectations for their students' success. While the entertaining allies appeared to enjoy teaching, Alan and Lan seemed to love it.

The following profile of Lan represents the Inspiring Cheerleaders. Given his strong evaluation by the students, Lan can be considered as an example of a very successful foreign TA.

## Profile of Lan

Lan is a native speaker of Chinese who taught a remedial math class, which met five days a week. When I observed the class, it was always well attended even though it met at 8:00 a.m.

Lan's English competence was the strongest of all the non-native speakers in the observational sample. Although there were occasional errors in his speech (e.g., articles, tense agreement, -s, etc.), there were no observable communication breakdowns. His pronunciation was good, and I could understand everything he said. He spoke at about the same rate as a native speaker.[5]

In addition to Lan's strong English proficiency, his nonverbal behavior was also near-native. He smiled a great deal, gestured and pointed as he explained, and maintained regular eye contact with the students, rarely talking toward the blackboard. His motions were graceful and confident. His posture and stance suggested that he was relaxed and open to the students.

Lan appeared to know his subject well. This is not surprising since he was a graduate student teaching remedial (high school level) math. But he was also familiar with his material. That is, he was apparently well organized and worked from a structured lesson plan. Furthermore, he shared that organization with the students, often explaining to them what he was planning to do in the rest of the lesson or even later in the week.

Beyond his linguistic and subject matter strengths, Lan had also mastered the role of a TA as a helper and ally. He was one of the most interactive TAs I observed. The regular class routine was for students to select difficult homework problems and volunteer to solve them at the blackboard. They then explained the solutions to their classmates. Lan was the only TA in the observational sample that involved the students to this extent. He also gave them a great deal of positive feedback when they were right and corrected them without belittling them when they were wrong. He used on-task humor and called individual students by name, which kept the tone of the class friendly but serious. He also used the inclusive forms *we* and *let's*, urged students to ask questions, praised their questions, encouraged them to do extra unassigned homework problems, and generally conveyed high positive expectations for their success in math. They, in turn, seemed to be very involved in his lessons—nodding, murmuring answers, overtly responding to his elicitations, correcting one another, or shaking their heads in disagreement.

On two occasions, students supplied spontaneous praise for Lan. At one observation he asked the students if the problems seemed easier, and a student said, "Yes, you've given us the tools to solve them." Following another observation, one of Lan's students passed me in the hall and said, "Isn't he wonderful? He makes me understand math as I've never understood it before." Lan seemed to have the equation for success as a math TA: know the material, speak English well, present the information in a clear and organized manner, get the students actively involved with the lesson, and show them that you care about them and believe in their potential for success.

## Summary of the TA Typology

The above typology can be summarized as follows:

Type 1: The active unintelligible TAs (e.g., Park) attempted to actually teach their students. However, the gaps in their language skills, especially their common pronunciation problems, compounded by the speed at which they spoke, were so serious as to impede communication.

Type 2: The mechanical problem solvers (e.g., Kwan) did not seem to engage in active teaching behaviors or to establish affective bonds with the students. Instead, they were rather passive and spoke very quietly. Their barebones teaching style primarily involved demonstrations of lab equipment and non-interactive solutions to homework problems.

Type 3: The knowledgeable helpers/casual friends, such as Lim, seemed to typify a basic, acceptable level of TA performance for the students. These TAs could all be understood, they all engaged in purposeful on-task teaching activities, and they established some positive affect in their classrooms.

Type 4: The entertaining allies were a small group consisting of only two native speaking TAs, Dan and Mark. Their teaching style, while purposeful, was characterized by consistent and active uses of humor and a "one-of-the-group" attitude. While the students were actively taught, they were also entertained by these TAs.

Type 5: The inspiring cheerleaders, another group of two TAs (Lan and Alan), generated infectious enthusiasm for the subject matter and high regard for the students. In addition to using well-organized and purposeful teaching behaviors, these two TAs communicated personal interest in the students as individuals and high expectations for their success.

Obviously these categories do not constitute an exhaustive list of all the possible TA types in U.S. universities. Allowing for individual variation, however, they do describe the majority of TAs observed in this study. But three teaching assistants did not seem to fit exactly into any of these categories. All three—Toshio, Curt, and Tim—were math TAs. But these TAs do not comprise a group themselves since they were quite different from one another, with the exception of one behavior pattern: They often either did not or could not help the students with the math assignments.

Tim was a first-time teaching assistant who had been awarded his TAship just before the beginning of the quarter. Although he was a graduate student in mathematics, he often could not solve the students' assigned homework problems. Yet he adopted a friendly attitude toward the students and commiserated with them on the difficulty of the material. Tim seems to have tried to approximate the role of a Type 3 TA, except that he was not a knowledgeable helper—he was only a casual friend.

Curt, in contrast, was not friendly to the students. His classroom style was condescending and haughty. He distanced himself from the students both physically and emotionally. For example, he stood with his back to the class as he explained or wrote on the blackboard, folding his arms across his chest when he faced the class. He sometimes used the inclusive pronouns *we* and *ours* to refer to himself and the math department faculty, rather than to himself and the students. Yet there was apparently little justification for Curt's aloofness. He often could not or did not solve the students' homework problems, and chose instead to lecture about math concepts that interested him.

While Curt had apparently mastered neither the subject matter nor the desired TA-student relationship, he had mastered a certain style of classroom discourse management which consisted largely of bravado and intimidation. It is possible that Curt represents a type of TA (or teacher) of which he was the only example among the TAs observed. That type could be called the patronizing egotist.

The third TA who did not fit in any of the five categories discussed above was Toshio, a native speaker of Japanese who taught a low-level math class for life science majors. Like Tim and Curt, he sometimes did not solve the students' homework problems, but he was more popular with the students. Toshio had partly adopted the role of TA as entertainer. His class periods were characterized by humorous anecdotes, personal history, and jokes. The students often laughed and they seemed fond of Toshio. However, while he was entertaining, he was not an ally to the students. For instance, he refused the students' request for an extra help session before an exam. And since his humor was seldom on-task, he did relatively little purposeful teaching. Unlike Dan and Mark, the entertaining allies, Toshio had not learned to balance his sense of humor with his primary responsibility—teaching math—or his unwritten responsibility—supporting the students.

## Concluding Remarks

What difference do these TA types make in teachers' and administrators' attempts to solve the foreign TA problem? When the students' evaluations of these TAs' teaching effectiveness were compared, a clear pattern of increasing mean scores was observed across the types, as shown in Table 1.

Table 1. *Students' evaluations of the teaching of five TA types*

| TA type | Mean score |
|---|---|
| Active unintelligible TAs (n = 3) | 36.8 |
| Mechanical problem solvers (n = 6) | 42.7 |
| Knowledgeable helpers/casual friends (n = 8) | 55.0 |
| Entertaining allies (n = 2) | 59.0 |
| Inspiring cheerleaders (n = 2) | 62.7 |

Thus, the active unintelligible TAs were rated the lowest by the students, followed by the mechanical problem solvers. There is a large gap between the mean score of the latter group and that of the third type, the knowledgeable helpers/casual friends. The entertaining allies and the inspiring cheerleaders were rated higher still, indicating the students' preference for their teaching styles over those of the lower rated groups.[6]

One of the responsibilities of TA trainers is to help foreign graduate students understand their role and the advantages and disadvantages of adopting any one role model over another. Used in conjunction with videotapes or role-plays, the descriptions of these TA types and the profiles which illustrate them could help novice TAs diagnose their own teaching and provide them with a clearer picture of students' reactions to various teaching styles. While long-term efforts may be required to improve foreign TAs' English proficiency, a better understanding of the TAs' role could lead to relatively quick behavioral changes in their classroom performance.

With the exception of the entertaining allies (which Toshio only resembled), foreign TAs are categorized as belonging to each of these TA types. This finding illustrates the obvious: non-native speakers are not automatically doomed to failure as TAs. Like their native speaking counterparts, they have options from which to choose as they undertake the TA role.

# Endnotes

1. This chapter is based on portions of the author's doctoral dissertation. Earlier drafts benefited from the constructive criticism of Frances Hinofotis, Russ Campbell, and Dan Shanahan, as well as the insight and patient scalpel of Harold Levine. For further details on the findings and methodology, see Bailey (1982).

2. On the Foreign Service Institute (FSI) Oral Interview, Park was rated as a "1 + ."

3. See Sadow and Maxwell (1983) for a good discussion of the first day of class. Those authors also provide a brief typology of American students.

4. Lim's FSI rating was a "2." (Kwan, whose profile is given as the example of a mechanical problem solver, declined to be interviewed.)

5. Lan's FSI rating was a "3."

6. A one-way analysis of variance revealed statistically significant differences among the mean scores of the five TA types, but Scheffes's test for a posteriori comparisons failed to detect the specific location(s) of these differences. It is possible that with a larger sample, clearer distinctions among the ratings of the TA types would emerge. For the present, the break between Type 2 looms the largest.

# References

Acton, W. 1980. Teaching English to teachers of undergraduates. Paper presented at the TESOL Convention, San Francisco, March 4-9.

Althen, G. 1981. *Manual for foreign teaching assistants*. Iowa City: Office of International Education and Services, University of Iowa.

Ard, J. and P. Rounds. 1982. Language use by foreign mathematics TAs. Paper presented at the TESOL Convention, Honolulu, May 1982.

Azevedo, M.M. 1976. Pre-service training for graduate teaching assistants. *Modern Language Journal* 60:254-257.

Bailey, K.M. 1977. The ESL service courses at UCLA: A progress report. In J. Povey (ed.), *Workpapers in teaching English as a second language*, Los Angeles: University of California.

——————— 1982a. Teaching in a second language: the communicative competence of non-native speaking teaching assistants (PhD dissertation in Applied Linguistics, University of California, Los Angeles). Ann Arbor: University Microfilms International.

——————— 1982b. The classroom communication problems of Asian teaching assistants. In C. Ward and D. Wren (eds.), *Selected Papers in TESOL*. Monterey: Monterey Institute of International Studies. 1:19-30.

———————1983a. Foreign teaching assistants at U.S. universities: Problems in interaction and communication. *TESOL Quarterly* 17:308-310.

——————— In press. If I had known then what I know now: performance testing of foreign teaching assistants. In P.C. Hauptman, R. LeBlanc, and M.B. Wesche (eds.), *Second language performance testing: Le testing de performance en langue seconde*. Ottawa: University of Ottawa.

Bailey, K.M. and R.N. Campbell. 1977. Selection, preparation and support of teaching assistants in a university English as a second language program. Paper presented at the TESOL Convention, Miami, April, 1977.

Bailey, N. 1978. Native accent and learning English as a foreign language. *International Review of Applied Linguistics* 16:227-240. August.

Barrus, J.L., T.R. Armstrong, M.M. Renfrew, and V.G. Garrard. 1974. Preparing teaching assistants. *Journal of College Science Teaching* 3:350-352.

Berdie, D.R., J.F. Anderson, M.S. Wenberg, and C.S. Price. 1976. Improving effectiveness of teaching assistants— undergraduates speak out. *Improving College Teaching*. 24:169-171.

Beukenkamp, E.J. 1981. The international teaching assistant's program at Cornell University. Unpublished manuscript (final report prepared by program staff), Ithaca, New York.

Birdwhistle, R.L. 1971. *Kinesics and context*. Philadelphia, PA: University of Pennsylvania Press.

Buckenmeyer, J.A. 1972. Preparing graduate assistants to teach. *Improving College and University Teaching* 20:142-144.

Cake, C. and L. Menasche. 1982. Improving the communication skills of foreign teaching assistants. Paper presented at the NAFSA Conference, Seattle (ED 225 373).

Centra, J.A. 1980. *Two studies on the validity of the Student Instructional Report* (SIR Report Number 4). Princeton, NJ: Educational Testing Service.

Cheney-Rice, S., E. Garate, and P. Shaw. 1980a. Pedagogy as E.S.P. Paper presented at the eleventh annual CATESOL State Conference, San Diego, April 18-20.

——————— 1980b. An integrated program for the training of non-native university teachers: a model and its consequences. Paper presented at the NAFSA Conference, St. Louis, May.

*Chronicle of Higher Education*. 1983. Florida legislature orders test of faculty members' English. July 7:2.

Clark, B.R. 1979. The development of international perspectives in American higher education. Conference on Internationalizing Higher Education, State University of New York, Buffalo, April.

Clark, J.L.D. and S.S. Swinton. 1979. *An exploration of speaking proficiency measures in the TOEFL context* (TOEFL Research Report 4). Princeton, NJ: Educational Testing Service.

—————————1980. *The Test of Spoken English as a measure of communicative ability in English-medium instructional settings* (TOEFL Research Report 7). Princeton, NJ: Educational Testing Service.

Cole, G.D., T. Campbell, A. Friedlander, R.H. Garner, A.D. Hagood, M.G. Hydak, J.G. Leonard, W.H. Macmillan, W.K. Rey, F.E. Ryerson, and R.F. Voss. (not dated). A university's commitment to its FTA Program. Unpublished manuscript, University of Alabama.

Dege, D.B. 1981. Format and evaluation of the cross-cultural component of a foreign teaching assistant training program. Paper presented at the Intercultural Division of the International Communication Association Conference, Minneapolis, May.

Douglas, M. 1975. *Implicit meanings: Essays in anthropology.* London: Routledge and Kegan Paul.

Educational Testing Service. 1980. TSE supervisor's manual. Princeton, NJ.

—————————1981. *TOEFL test and score manual.* Princeton, NJ.

—————————1982. *Test of Spoken English: Manual for score users.* Princeton, NJ.

—————————1982. *TSE examinee handbook and sample questions.* Princeton, NJ.

Ferguson, N. 1978. Test N73: Instantaneous evaluation of speaking ability. *International Review of Applied Linguistics* 16:340-349. November.

Fisher, M. (ed.), 1981. Teaching at Stanford: An introductory handbook. Stanford: Center for Teaching and Learning.

Franck, M. and M. De Sousa. 1980. Report on Rhetoric 298: teaching practicum for foreign students. Unpublished manuscript, Teaching Resources Center, University of California, Davis.

Friedman, C.B. and R. Bier. 1981. Foreign students as teaching assistants: the process used to screen and test potential teaching assistants. Paper presented at the NAFSA Conference, Region VI, Bloomington, Indiana, Nov. 8-10.

—————————— 1982. Certifying the English proficiency of foreign teaching assistants: the problem and the process. In P. Bjarkman (ed.), *New directions for TESOL: Proceedings of the Second Midwest Regional TESOL Conference.*

Gitter, A. G., H. Black, and A. Goldman. 1978. Role of nonverbal communication in the perception of leadership. *Perceptual and Motor Skills* 40:463-466. April.

Goepper, J.B. and M. Knorre. 1980. Pre- and in-service training of graduate teaching assistants. *Modern Language Journal* 64:446-450.

Gordon, T. 1973. P.E.T.: *Parent effectiveness training.* New York: Peter H. Wyden, Inc.

Graham, J.A. and M. Argyle. 1975. A cross-cultural study of the communication of extra-verbal meaning by gestures. *Journal of Human Movement Studies* 1:33-39. March.

Gumperz, J.J., T.C. Jupp and C. Roberts. 1979. Crosstalk: A study of cross-cultural communication. Southall: The National Center for Industrial Training.

Gurnick, D. 1981. And gladly would he learn and gladly teach: The difficult role of the teaching assistant at UCLA. *The TA at UCLA Newsletter* 1:3.

Hagiwara, M.P. 1976. The training of graduate teaching assistants: Past, present and future. *ADFL Bulletin* 7:7-12. Hall, E.T. 1959. *The silent language.* Greenwich, CT: Fawcett Publications.

Henry, J. 1960. A cross-cultural survey of education. *Current Anthropology* 1:285-286.

Heyde Parsons, A. and L. Szelagowski. 1983. Communication skills for the international teaching associate at Ohio University. *NAFSA Newsletter* March: 114-116 and 122.

Hinofotis, F.B. 1976. An investigation of the concurrent validity of cloze testing as a measure of overall proficiency in English as a second language. Unpublished doctoral dissertation, Southern Illinois University.

Hinofotis, F.B. and K.M. Bailey. 1978. Course development: oral communication for advanced university ESL students. In J. Povey (ed.), *Workpapers in teaching English as a second language.* Los Angeles: University of California. 12:7-20.

—————————— 1980. American undergraduates' reactions to the communication skills of foreign teaching assistants. In J.C. Fisher, M.A. Clarke, and J. Schachter (eds.), *On TESOL '80— Building bridges: Research and practice in teaching English as a second language.* Washington, D.C.: TESOL, 120 133.

Hinofotis, F.B., K.M. Bailey, and S.L. Stern. 1978. A progress report on English 34: Oral communication for foreign students. Unpublished manuscript. Department of English (TESL Section), University of California, Los Angeles.

—————————— 1979. Assessing improvement in oral communication: raters' perceptions of change. In J. Povey (ed.), *Workpapers in teaching English as a second language*. Los Angeles: University of California. 13:27-39.

—————— 1981. Assessing the oral proficiency of prospective foreign teaching assistants: Instrument development. In A. Palmer, P.J.M. Groot, and G. Trosper (eds.), *Selected papers from the Colloquium for Oral Proficiency Testing at the 1979 TESOL Convention*. Washington, D.C.: TESOL.

Horn, N.E. 1980. Course report—TA ESL: A pilot project funded by Instructional Development. Unpublished manuscript, Instructional Development Office, University of California, Santa Barbara.

Hymes, D. (ed.), 1972. *Reinventing anthropology*. New York: Pantheon Books.

*International students at the University of Minnesota*. 1982. Unpublished report prepared by a presidentially appointed administrative committee, University of Minnesota.

Jacobs, L.C. and C.B. Friedman. Forthcoming. Comparison of student achievement in classes taught by native and foreign teaching assistants. Bloomington, IN: Bureau of Evaluative Studies and Testing, Indiana University.

Kaplan, R.B. 1966. Cultural thought patterns in intercultural education. *Language Learning* 16:1-20.

Keesing, F.M. 1958. *Cultural anthropology: The science of custom*. New York: Holt, Rinehart and Winston.

Keller, E. and S.T. Warner. 1976. *Gambits: Conversational tools*. Ottawa: Minister of Supply and Services, Canada.

——————1979. *Gambits 2: Conversational tools*. Ottawa: Public Services Commission of Canada.

Kelley, J. 1982. Foreign teachers bring language problems to U.S. campuses. *Los Angeles Times*, June 18, Part I-C:12.

Keye, Z.A. 1981. An exploratory study of students' written responses to foreign teaching assistant presentations. *Dissertation Abstracts International* 41.

Kim, K.H. 1977. Misunderstandings in nonverbal communication: America and Korea. *Papers in Linguistics* 10:1-22.

Knapp, M.L. 1972. The effects of environment and space on human communication. *Nonverbal communication and human interaction*. New York: Holt, Rinehart and Winston.

Kneller, G. F. 1965. *Educational anthropology*. New York: John Wiley & Sons, Inc.

Lado, R. 1957. *Linguistics across cultures*. Ann Arbor: University of Michigan Press.

Landa, M. and W. Perry. 1980. Classroom communication for foreign teaching assistants. *NAFSA Newsletter*. 31:145 and 147.

Levine, D.R. and M.B. Adelman. 1982. *Beyond language: Intercultural communication for English as a second language*. Englewood Cliffs, NJ: Prentice-Hall.

Lewis, W.R. and C.C. Orvis. 1973. A training system for graduate student instructors of introductory economics at the University of Minnesota. *Journal of Economic Education* 5:38-46. Lewthwaite, R. 1981. The students' teacher, the professors' assistant. *The TA at UCLA Newsletter* 7:5.

Livesley, W.J. and D.B. Bromley. 1973. *Person perception in childhood and adolescence*. London: John Wiley and Sons, Ltd.

Livingston, S. A. and M. J. Zieky. 1982. *Passing scores: A manual for setting standards of performance on educational and occupational tests*. Princeton, NJ: Educational Testing Service.

Lnenicka, W. J. 1972. Are teaching assistants teachers? *Improving College and University Teaching* 20:97.

Lurie, L. 1981. Personalizing the university: An undergraduate's view of TAs. *The TA at UCLA Newsletter* 7:4.

Macer, J. 1982. Focus on Asian teaching assistants: a general profile and a look at cultural, linguistic and pedagogical differences. Paper presented at the 1982 NAFSA Conference, Seattle, May.

Mackay, R. and M. Bosquet. 1981. LSP curriculum development— From policy to practice. In R. Mackay and J.D. Palmer (eds.), *Languages for specific purposes: Program design and evaluation*. Rowley, MA: Newbury House.

McKeachie, W.J. 1978. *Teaching tips: A guidebook for the beginning college teacher*, 7th ed., Lexington, MA: Heath.

McMahan, E.M. 1976. Nonverbal communication as a function of attribution in impression formation. *Communication Monographs* 43. November.

Mestenhauser, J., W. Perry, M. Paige, M. Landa, S. Brutsch, D. Dege, K. Doyle, S. Gillette, G. Hughes, R. Judy, Z. Keye, K. Murphy, J. Smith, K. Vandersluis, and J. Wendt. 1980. *Report of a special course for foreign student teaching assistants to improve their classroom effectiveness.* Minneapolis: University of Minnesota International Students Adviser's Office and Program in English as a Second Language.

Metraux, R. 1963. Implicit and explicit values in growth, education and teaching as related to development. In G.D. Spindler (ed.), *Education and culture: Anthropological approaches.* New York: Holt, Rinehart and Winston.

Montgomery, M. 1976. The structure of lectures. Unpublished master's thesis, University of Birmingham.

Morley, J. 1979. *Improving spoken English: An intensive program in perception, pronunciation, practice in context.* Ann Arbor, MI: University of Michigan Press.

Muhlestein, L.D. and B. DeFacio. 1974. Teaching graduate teaching assistants to teach. *American Journal of Physics* 42:384-386.

Munby, J. 1978. *Communicative syllabus design.* Cambridge: Cambridge University Press.

Orth, J.L. 1983. Language attitudes and naive listeners' evaluations of speaking proficiency: The case of foreign teaching assistants. Paper presented at the Annual TESOL Convention, Toronto.

Palmer, H.E. and H.V. Redman. 1969. *This language-learning business.* London: Oxford University Press.

Powers, D.E. and C.W. Stansfield. 1983. *The Test of Spoken English as a measure of communicative ability in the health professions: Validation and standard setting* (TOEFL Research Report 13). Princeton, NJ: Educational Testing Service.

Rodman, G. R. 1978. *Public speaking: A guide to message preparation.* New York: Holt, Rinehart and Winston.

Rose, C. 1972. An in-service program for teaching assistants. *Improving College and University Teaching* 20:100-102.

Russo, G. 1983. The training of teaching assistants. *Expanding communication.* New York: Harcourt, Brace, Jovanovich, 139-148.

Sadow, S.A. and M. A. Maxwell. 1983. The foreign teaching assistant and the culture of the American university class. In M.A. Clarke and J. Handscombe (eds.), *On TESOL '82—Pacific perspectives on language learning and teaching.* Washington, D.C.: TESOL.

*San Francisco Examiner.* 1978. Language lessons for teacher aides. May 6, Section E:4.

Shaw, E. 1982. No comprende! Foreign TAs try to cope with English. *The Daily Pennsylvanian,* February 15, 1982:3.

Siebring, B.R. 1972. A training program for teaching assistants. *Improving College and University Teaching* 20:98-99.

Simon, S.B., L.W. Howe, and H. Kirschenbaum. 1972. *Values clarification: A handbook of practical strategies for teachers and students.* New York: Hart Publishing Company, Inc.

Sledd, J. 1959. *A short introduction to English grammar.* Glenview, Illinois: Scott, Foresman and Co.

Sollenberger, H.E. 1978. Development and current use of the FSI Oral Interview Test. In J.L.D. Clark (ed.), *Direct testing of speaking proficiency: Theory and application.* Princeton, NJ: Educational Testing Service.

Smith, R.M. 1982. An intensive summer workshop for foreign teaching assistants: a pilot project. *TESOL Newsletter.* 16:31.

Staton-Spicer, A.Q. and J.L. Nyquist. 1979. Improving the teaching effectiveness of graduate teaching assistants. *Communication Education* 28:199-205.

Stockdale, D.L. and Z.S. Wochok. 1974. Training TAs to teach. *Journal of College Science Teaching* 3:345-349.

Swanbeck, H. 1981. Foreign TAs experience communication gap in classroom. *Daily Bruin,* October 26, 1981:1, 9, and 10.

*TSE examinee handbook and sample questions.* 1982. Princeton, NJ: Educational Testing Service.

*TSE supervisor's manual.* 1980. Princeton, NJ: Educational Testing Service.

Timmerman, M. 1981. Foreign profs' language barrier irritates students. *Daily Bruin*, May 4, 1981.

Tu, N. 1983. A comparison of the spoken discourse of eight native and non-native speaking physics TAs. Unpublished master's thesis, University of California, Los Angeles.

Tylor, E.B. 1872. *Primitive culture*. London: John Murray.

van Ek, J. 1976. *The threshold level for modern language learning in schools*. London: Longman Group Ltd.

Von Blum, P. 1981. Utopian reflections about teaching assistants. *The TA at UCLA Newsletter* 7:1.

Weinberg, S. B. 1979. Measurement of communication aspects of group cohesion. *Journal of Applied Communication*. April.

Weinberg, S. B., L. J. Smotroff and J. C. Pecke. 1978. Communication factors of group leadership. *Journal of Applied Communication Research* 6:20.

Wilds, C. P. 1975. The oral interview test. In R. Jones and B. Spolsky (eds.), *Testing language proficiency*. Arlington, VA: Center for Applied Linguistics.

Wilkins, D. A. 1977. *Notional syllabi*. Oxford: Oxford University Press.

Young, R. and Y. Wang. 1982. Effective TAing program: A program report. Unpublished manuscript, Foundation for Scholarly Exchange, Taipei.

# Contributors

Kathleen M. Bailey completed an M.A. in TESL and a Ph.D. in Applied Linguistics at UCLA. Her doctoral dissertation dealt with the communicative competence of non-native speaking TAs. She is currently the Director of the TESOL M.A. Program and Chairperson of the American Language and Culture Division at the Monterey Institute of International Studies.

Rodney J. Ballard received an M.A. in Middle Eastern Languages from Columbia University in 1973. He is currently Director of the Test of Spoken English Program at Educational Testing Service, Princeton, New Jersey.

Donna Brinton is an Adjunct Lecturer and Audio-Visual Consultant with the ESL Section at UCLA. She is a graduate of the UCLA TESL program, and has served in her current capacity since 1979. She has taught ESL through the American Language Center at UCLA Extension, at Marymount Palos Verdes College, and in Germany. She is the co-author (with Regina Neuman) of *Getting Along: English Grammar and Writing*, Prentice Hall, 1981.

Elena M. Garate is the Assistant Director of the Office of International Students and Scholars at the University of Southern California, where she completed her Ph.D. in International Education and was one of the originators of USC's training program for international teaching assistants. She also authored the videotape series, "The NAFSA Co-op Program: Intercultural Inservice Training for University Communities."

William Gaskill is the Academic Coordinator of the UCLA Extension American Language Center. He is also a Ph.D. candidate in the UCLA Program in Applied Linguistics. His dissertation, a process-oriented study of composing in a second language, focuses on the revisions that ESL students make on in-class compositions. He is especially interested in the teaching of writing to ESL students and in ESL curriculum development.

Frances B. Hinofotis is an assistant professor of English at UCLA, where she has conducted research on foreign teaching assistants and taught an advanced oral communications course geared for prospective TAs. Her primary research interests are in the area of oral language proficiency testing.

Mark Landa is the Director of the English Program for International Students at the University of Minnesota. He has developed video materials for speaking courses that he teaches in the Univesity's Extension Division. He has also taught in Japan, China, Scotland and the Netherlands.

William Perry is a full-time instructor at the University of Wisconsin-Madison. He has taught ESL at the University of Minnesota and EFL in Yugoslavia as a Fulbright Junior Lecturer. He has been involved in curriculum development in courses for foreign TAs and also in research on the relationship between English language test performance and the academic performance of foreign graduate students.

Frank Pialorsi is an Associate Professor of English and Director of the Center for English as a Second Language at the University of Arizona, where he completed a Ph.D. in Educational Anthropology and designed a special training program for foreign TAs. He has held Fulbright positions in Greece, Japan, and Korea.

Donna Steed Rice is Assistant Director for Intensive Programs and Lecturer in ESL at the Intensive English Language Institute, SUNY/Buffalo. She is a former Visiting Professor and Resident Director of the SUNY/Buffalo English Training Center at the Beijing Foreign Languages Institute Branch School.

Peter A. Shaw has taught English and trained teachers in Europe, Nigeria, Mexico, and California. He completed his Ph.D. in Linguistics (Applied Emphasis) at the University of Southern California, where he helped to establish and teach the intensive orientation program for international teaching assistants. He is now the director of the Intensive English Program at the Monterey Institute of International Studies.

Charles W. Stansfield received his Ph.D. in Foreign/Second Language Education in 1973. He is now the Research Coordinator for the TOEFL Program at Educational Testing Service. Previously, he served as director of the Test of Spoken English Program and has published widely on second language teaching and testing.

Nina J. Turitz received her M.S. in Applied Linguistics from Georgetown University in 1978. She taught in and coordinated ESL courses at the American Language Academy in Washington, D.C., in addition to teaching EFL in Paris. Ms. Turitz is currently an instructor at the Maryland English Institute, University of Maryland/College Park.

Jean Zukowski/Faust completed her M.A. and Ph.D. at the University of Arizona, where she is now an Assistant Professor of English. She taught the first experimental course for foreign TAs there and now teaches courses in

TESOL methodology and grammar. Dr. Zukowski/Faust spent eight years in Turkey, three of them with the Peace Corps. She has published three books with Holt, Rinehart and Winston.